ESSENTIAL
LANZAROTE AND
FUERTEVENTURA

Original text by Andrew Sanger
Updated by Jane Egginton

© AA Media Limited 2009
First published 2007
Information verified and updated 2009. Reprinted September 2011.

ISBN: 978-0-7495-6013-3

Published by AA Publishing, a trading name of AA Media Limited, whose registered office is Fanum House, Basing View, Basingstoke, Hampshire RG21 4EA. Registered number 06112600.

Colour separation: MRM Graphics Ltd. Printed and bound in Italy by Printer Trento S.r.l.

Find out more about AA Publishing and the wide range of services the AA provides by visiting our website at theAA.com/shop

A04736
Maps in this title produced from mapping © MAIRDUMONT/Falk Verlag 2011

About this book

This book is divided into five sections.

The essence of Lanzarote and Fuerteventura pages 6–19
Introduction; Features; Food and drink; Short break including the 10 Essentials

Planning pages 20–33
Before you go; Getting there; Getting around; Being there

Best places to see pages 34–55
The unmissable highlights of any visit to Lanzarote and Fuerteventura

Best things to do pages 56–79
Good places to have lunch; stunning views; places to take the children; boat excursions and more

Exploring pages 80–186
The best places to visit in Lanzarote and Fuerteventura, organized by area

Maps
All map references are to the maps on the covers. For example, Arrecife has the reference ➕ 7D – indicating the grid square in which it is to be found

Admission prices
Inexpensive (under €3)
Moderate (€3–€6)
Expensive (over €6)

Hotel prices
Price are per room per night:
€ budget (under €65);
€€ moderate (€65–€90);
€€€ expensive to luxury (over €90)

Restaurant prices
Price for a three-course meal per person without drinks:
€ budget (under €15);
€€ moderate (€15–€30);
€€€ expensive (over €30)

Contents

BEST THINGS TO DO

EXPLORING...

56 – 79   80 – 186

The essence of...

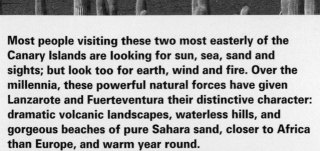

Most people visiting these two most easterly of the
Canary Islands are looking for sun, sea, sand and
sights; but look too for earth, wind and fire. Over the
millennia, these powerful natural forces have given
Lanzarote and Fuerteventura their distinctive character:
dramatic volcanic landscapes, waterless hills, and
gorgeous beaches of pure Sahara sand, closer to Africa
than Europe, and warm year round.

These islands have largely avoided the over-
development and 'lager lout' culture of many other
popular sunshine destinations. Low-key family resorts,
well-equipped small complexes, inland villas with
pools, and an unspoiled blue and gold coastline give
Lanzarote and Fuerteventura a civilized air.

features

There's something in the harsh paradox of these volcanic islands that thrills the soul. The austere, timeless emptiness; the dryness recalling the nearby Sahara; the menacing hint of nature's enduring power; the overwhelming solitude and silence – all these beckon, yet defy man to make a home here.

These islands are indeed very thinly populated. Fuerteventura's average of 12 people per square kilometre is the lowest in the Canaries, and even that figure gives no clue to the sense of space, for almost everyone lives in just one place – Puerto del Rosario. Lanzarote's case, while not quite as extreme, is similar: most people live in Arrecife.

Yet these are not desert islands, but Spanish territories with agriculture, art, history, traditions and folkore, culture and cuisine. They are also holiday lands with hotels, beaches and hire cars.

That is the paradox. The destructive forces of nature – exemplified by the eruption of Timanfaya volcano in the 1730s, when burning rock rained on Lanzarote and swept away fields and villages that islanders had nurtured for centuries – have themselves now been harnessed by man's own great powers of survival and imagination. Getting

visitors to pay to see the volcanoes, and using the heat of the Fire Mountains to barbecue steaks, is a victory of sorts. A temporary one, perhaps, for the volcanoes may erupt again one day, and the sands continue to blow over from Africa.

PEOPLE
● Some 130,000 people live on Lanzarote and about 90,000 on Fuerteventura. On both islands, over half the population live in their respective capital.
● Ethnically the islanders are thought to be a mix of Berber, Arab, Norman and Spanish.
● Fuerteventura natives are known as *mahoreros*, after the goatskin shoes of their ancestors, while Lanzaroteños are called *conejeros*, meaning rabbit hunters.

CLIMATE
● Unlike the other Canaries, these two islands remain practically rain-free all year round, though there can be winter cloud. Any rain normally falls between October and March, with a total annual precipitation of 140mm (5.5 inches).
● Average daytime temperatures remain almost constant at around 21°C (70°F) on Lanzarote, 19°C (66°F) on Fuerteventura all year round.

SIZE
● The second largest of the Canaries, Fuerteventura is only slightly smaller than Tenerife. At 1,731sq km (668sq miles), it is over twice the size of Lanzarote's 813sq km (314sq miles).

LANGUAGE
● Spanish is the language of the Canaries, but islanders also have a patois of their own. English is widely spoken (though not usually very well), especially at resorts and tourist attractions.

food & drink

These islands' distinct identities and rich histories have produced a wonderful, regional cuisine, typified by hearty stews and simple barbecued fish. For visitors who want to experience the real character and gastronomy of Lanzarote and Fuerteventura, there's plenty of delicious local food to be enjoyed. While the informal eateries in beach resorts do tend to focus on international favourites, most inland restaurants offer traditional *típico* cuisine.

MOJO

One of the most genuinely Canarian words on the menu is *mojo*. Meat, fish and vegetables may all be served *con mojo* – with *mojo* – the spicy dipping sauce that comes in different versions, according to what it accompanies. The two main types are *mojo verde* (green *mojo*) made with parsley, garlic and coriander giving a cool, sharp flavour, and *mojo rojo*, the spicier, red sauce made with chillies and peppers.

GOFIO

The other most distinctively Canarian food is *gofio*. This staple of the Guanche diet is still very much in use. A rough roasted wholemeal flour (usually of maize, but possibly also of barley, wheat or even chickpeas), it appears in soups, as a sort of polenta, as a paste mixed with vegetables, or as breads, cakes and puddings. *Flan gofio*, which resembles semolina pudding, has interesting African undertones. The people of Lanzarote and Fuerteventura are fond of hearty

meat stews – sometimes with misleading names like Lanzarote's *potaje de berros* (watercress soup), in which the greenery may be barely discernible. Such rich, savoury soup-stews, usually combining several meats, including pork and rabbit, with chickpeas and vegetables and often thickened with *gofio*, are the main

speciality; *rancho canario* and *puchero* (similar to French cassoulet) are typical, and especially popular for Sunday lunch. *El cocido* is Fuerteventura's version of these traditional Canarian *garbanzos compuestos* (chickpea stews). Rabbit *(conejo)* is an especially popular and inexpensive ingredient on Lanzarote.

FISH

Fish soups include the well-known Canarian *sancocho*, a thick stew of salted fish and vegetables. Start your meal with *gambas al ajillo*, shrimps in garlic-rich olive oil, or *pulpo*, octopus. Main dishes tend to be plain and simple, such as grilled or fried fresh fish.

VEGETABLES

Vegetarians beware – *potaje* (vegetable stew) usually contains some meat. Thanks in part to the obvious difficulties of cultivation in this volcanic landscape, vegetables don't feature strongly in local specialities. But there are notable exceptions, in particular *cebollas* (onions), *batatas* (sweet

potatoes) and tasty small *papas* (the local name for potatoes), which usually appear as *papas arrugadas*. Literally 'wrinkly potatoes', these are delectable new potatoes cooked in their skins with plenty of salt until the water has completely boiled away, sometimes served with a heavy sprinkling of crunchy rock salt – and *mojo*. Eat them by hand. *Batatas con mojo*, sweet potatoes in hot sauce, are an interesting alternative.

DESSERTS

Finish with a thick, chocolatey dessert, or corn cakes and syrup. Popular *frangollo* is made of *gofio* and dried fruit doused in syrup. Bananas are readily available, and for dessert are usually served fried or as *bienmesabe* – baked with chocolate and cream.

CHEESE

Cheesemaking is a local craft. On Fuerteventura, the islanders are proud of their traditional *majorero* goat's cheese, with its milky white colour and nutty flavour, a version of which is made on Lanzarote.

MALVASIA

While other Canary Islands may produce wine, few can compete with Lanzarote's fine malvasia. Made of the grape that normally produces malmsey, Lanzarote's version – from the volcanic vineyards of La Geria – has a delicious crisp fruity dryness, full of light and flavour. Local wines can be purchased from shops and enjoyed in restaurants throughout the islands.

short break

If you have only a short time to visit Lanzarote and Fuerteventura and would like to take home some unforgettable memories, you can do something local and capture the real flavour of the islands. The following suggestions are a range of sights and experiences that won't take very long and will make your visit very special.

● **See twigs burst into flame** on Islote de Hilario (➤ 44–45). This unforgettable volcanic phenomenon is demonstrated by park rangers at Timanfaya National Park on Lanzarote. When brushwood is dropped into a fissure the scorching ground temperature instantly ignites it and when water is emptied into the ground it transforms into a scalding geyser.

● **Take the bus tour** from Islote de Hilario. Coaches depart continuously on the Ruta de los Volcanes (Route of the Volcanoes) tour. This 40-minute trip, taking in the highlights of the central part of the Timanfaya National Park, is a great way to get into the very heart of volcano country; make sure you get a window seat on the bus (➤ 130–131).

THE ESSENCE OF LANZAROTE AND FUERTEVENTURA

● **Visit the Fundación César Manrique.** The genius and flair of the man who made Lanzarote great can be felt in his former home (➤ 42–43) at Taro de Tahíche. This amazing house, constructed in a string of volcanic holes in the ground, is now an important art gallery. Don't miss the giant mural in the beautiful gardens.

● **Go to the Jameos del Agua** during the day just to gaze and wonder at this spectacular creation, or in the evening for a night out or dining experience in an amazing setting (➤ 46–47).

● **Sunbathe on a golden beach,** not the grainy black stuff more typical of the other Canary Islands. Lanzarote and Fuerteventura have wide stretches of fine pale sand that are a delight for children, sun worshippers and watersport enthusiasts.

● **Eat *papas arrugadas con mojo*.** These small new potatoes boiled in, and served with, a generous sprinkling of sea salt, are ultra-tasty and one of the best local specialities (➤ 14–15). *Mojo* is a traditional Canarian piquant sauce.

● **Drink local wine.** If you think a barren volcanic landscape is not the best place to grow grapes, you haven't tried Lanzarote's cool, crisp and dry

Malvasia white wines. You can taste as many as you like at the island's *bodegas* (wineries); pick up the booklet *Tourism for Wine Lovers* from the tourist office that gives details of the island's *bodegas*. A good place to buy island wines is the shop at the Monumento al Campesino (➤ 122–123).

● **Walk 10 paces on the volcanic *malpaís*.** To understand just how unworkable this land is, try walking on it. The best place to try this is the bleak, black volcanic fields of La Geria (➤ 142), where it's easy to pull over to the side of the road and get out of the car. The Lanzarote *malpaís* has good examples of all the various kinds of volcanic material thrown forth by volcanoes: ash and dust particles; small solid particles; lightweight fragments of rock shot through with air bubbles; large pieces of solid rock scattered about and most familiar of all – lava.

● **Walk on giant sand dunes.** East of Lanzarote's Playa Blanca, or in Fuerteventura's Dunes Natural Park or Pared Isthmus, stroll on the rolling, drifting desert sandscapes. It is possible to escape from the sight and sound of traffic and hotels, and imagine yourself in a Lawrence-of-Arabia world.

● **Take a trip to another island.** Whether you're on Lanzarote or Fuerteventura, it's worth making a day trip to see the sights the other has to offer. It's also fun to explore the less touristy islands of Isla Graciosa (➤ 92–95), 2km (1.2 miles) off Lanzarote, or Isla de Lobos (➤ 172), 3km (2 miles) off Fuerteventura.

Planning

Before you go

WHEN TO GO

JAN	FEB	MAR	APR	MAY	JUN	JUL	AUG	SEP	OCT	NOV	DEC
21°C	21°C	23°C	24°C	25°C	26°C	28°C	29°C	29°C	27°C	24°C	21°C
70°F	70°F	73°F	75°F	77°F	79°F	82°F	84°F	84°F	81°F	75°F	70°F

🌧️ 🌧️ ☀️ ☀️ ☀️ ☀️ ☀️ ☀️ ☀️ 🌧️ 🌧️ 🌧️

⬤ High season ⬤ Low season

Temperatures are the average daily maximum for each month. Minimum temperatures rarely drop below 15°C (59°F); average temperatures range from 19°C (66°F) in winter to 26°C (79°F) in summer. Most of the rain falls in the north of Lanzarote and there is occasional snow in the mountains.

Although windy on the island of Fuerteventura, most of the time the air is clear and comes from the north. However, when the sirocco – the dry wind from the east – blows it brings dust as well as heat. The sirocco blows for short spells at a time, and mainly in winter.

The high season runs from November to April, with a second peak in July and August. The quietest months are May, June, September and October.

WHAT YOU NEED

		UK	Germany	USA	Netherlands	Spain
●	Required					
○	Suggested					
▲	Not required					

Some countries require a passport to remain valid for a minimum period (usually at least six months) beyond the date of entry – contact their consulate or embassy or your travel agent for details.

	UK	Germany	USA	Netherlands	Spain
Passport/National Identity Card	●	●	●	●	●
Visa (regulations can change – check before you travel)	▲	▲	▲	▲	▲
Onward or Return Ticket	▲	▲	○	▲	▲
Health Inoculations (tetanus and polio)	▲	▲	▲	▲	▲
Health Documentation (► 23, Health Insurance)	▲	▲	▲	▲	▲
Travel Insurance	○	○	○	○	○
Driving Licence (national)	●	●	●	●	●
Health Insurance	○	○	○	○	○

WEBSITES

- Official tourist offices
www.turismolanzarote.com
www.fuerteventuraturismo.com
- Other good sites
www.lanzaroteguidebook.com

www.lanzaroteisland.com
www.spain-lanzarote.com
www.fuerteventura.com
www.fuerteventurainfo.com

TOURIST OFFICES AT HOME

In the UK Spanish National Tourist Office, PO Box 4009, London, W1A 6NB; ☎ (020) 7486 8077 (am only); www.spain.info

In the USA Spanish National Tourist Office, 666 Fifth Avenue, 35th floor, New York, NY 10103 ☎ (212) 265

8822; www.okspain.org
Other SNTOs in Chicago, Los Angeles and Miami

In Canada Spanish National Tourist Office, 2 Bloor St W, Suite 3402, Toronto, Ontario, M4W 3E2 ☎ (416) 961 3131; www.tourspain.toronto.on.ca

HEALTH INSURANCE

EU nationals receive free medical treatment with the relevant documentation (European Health Insurance Card for UK nationals). German- and English-speaking doctors practise at private Clinic Dr Mager, 37 Avenida de las Playas, Puerto del Carmen (tel: 928 51 26 11). There are also branches in Costa Teguise and Playa Blanca.

Emergency dental treatment is expensive but is covered by most medical insurance (but not by EHIC). Keep bills for insurance claims.

TIME DIFFERENCES

GMT	Canaries	Germany	USA (NY)	Netherlands	Spain
12 noon	12 noon	1PM	7AM	1PM	1PM

Lanzarote and Fuerteventura (and all the Canary Islands) follow Greenwich Mean Time (GMT), but from the last Sunday in March – when clocks are put forward one hour – until the Saturday before the last Sunday in October, summer time operates (GMT+1).

NATIONAL HOLIDAYS

1 January *Año Nuevo* (New Year's Day)

6 January *Epifanía* (Epiphany)

March/April *Pascua* (Easter) Thu, Fri, Sun of Easter Week

1 May *Día del Trabajo* (Labour Day)

30 May *Día de las Canarias* (Canary Islands' Day)

15 August *Asunción* (Assumption)

12 October *Día de la Hispanidad* (National Day)

1 November *Día de la Todos los Santos* (All Saints' Day)

6 December *Día de la Constitución* (Constitution Day)

8 December *Inmaculada Concepción* (Immaculate Conception)

25 December *Navidad* (Christmas Day)

WHAT'S ON WHEN

January *Cabalgata de los Reyes Magos Festival* (Three Kings Parade, 5 Jan): Teguise, Lanzarote.

February *Fiesta de Nuestra Señora de Candelaria* (Candlemas, 2 Feb): a big festival and pilgrimage in certain villages, for example Gran Tarajal and La Oliva on Fuerteventura.

Carnaval (two weeks, dates vary each year): especially exuberant in Arrecife, Lanzarote and Corralejo, Fuerteventura.

March/April *Easter:* look out for religious processions all over the islands during Easter Week.

May *Fiestas* on Fuerteventura include: Tarajalejo (8 May); La Lajita (13 May).

Ironman (3rd weekend): international triathlon on Lanzarote.

June *Fiesta de San Juan* (night of 23 and 24 Jun): celebrating the midsummer, Haría, Lanzarote, with bonfires all over the island.

Corpus Christi: Arrecife and Haría, Lanzarote. Patterns of coloured salt are used to decorate the ground.

July *Fiesta de Nuestra Señora de Regla* (2 Jul): Pájara, Fuerteventura.

Fiesta de San Buenaventura (14 Jul): Betancuria, Fuerteventura. Festival to honour the town's patron saint and the incorporation of the island into Spain.

Fiesta de Nuestra Señora del Carmen (16 Jul): Teguise, La Graciosa, Arrecife and Puerto del Carmen on Lanzarote; Corralejo and Morro Jable on Fuerteventura. Processions, street fairs and folkloric shows.

Fiesta (last Sat in Jul): La Pared, Fuerteventura. On the last Saturday fishing boats are put out to sea with charmingly decorated effigies of the saints on board.

August *Fiesta de San Ginés* (for a week from 25 Aug): everywhere, but especially Arrecife, Lanzarote. Processions, parades and traditional dancing in the streets.

Semana de la Juventud (Youth Week, mid-Aug onwards): Gran Tarajal, Fuerteventura.

September *Fiesta de Nuestra Señora de Antigua* (8 Sep): in honour of Antigua's patron saint, Fuerteventura.

Virgen de los Volcanes (15 Sep): pilgrimage to Mancha Blanca, Lanzarote.

Fiesta de Nuestra Señora de la Peña (3rd Sat): Vega de Río Palmas, Fuerteventura.

Fiesta de San Miguel (29 Sep): Tuineje, Fuerteventura.

October *Visual Music Festival* (whole month): in Jameos del Agua and Cueva de los Verdes, Lanzarote.

Fiesta de Nuestra Señora del Rosario (7 Oct): Puerto del Rosario, Fuerteventura.

Battle of Tamacita (13 Oct): Tuineje, Fuerteventura.

November *International Kite Festival* (2nd weekend): La Playa del Burro, Fuerteventura.

December *Christmas:* nativity plays and processions take place all over the Canary Islands.

Getting there

BY AIR

Arrecife Airport

6km (4 miles) to city centre

N/A

20 minutes

10 minutes

Puerto del Rosario Airport

5km (3 miles) to city centre

N/A

15 minutes

8 minutes

All flights to Lanzarote arrive at Arrecife airport (tel: 928 84 60 00; www.aena.es), which lies between Arrecife (6km/4 miles away) and Puerto del Carmen (10km/6 miles).

Flights to Fuerteventura arrive at Puerto del Rosario's small airport (tel: 928 86 06 04; www.aena.es), which lies between the island's capital (5km/3 miles away) and Caleta de Fuste (8km/5 miles).

There are numerous charter flights to Lanzarote and Fuerteventura throughout the year from London and other European cities. Most seats are sold by tour operators as part of a package holiday; it is possible to buy flight-only deals, although you are usually restricted to a period of either 7 or 14 days. EasyJet (www.easyjet.com) flies direct from London Gatwick to Lanzarote, and the Spanish airline Iberia (www.iberia.com) operates flights from London to Lanzarote and Fuerteventura via Madrid.

INTER-ISLAND TRAVEL

By air Binter Canarias (tel: 902 39 13 92; www.binternet.com) offers daily flights from Lanzarote and Fuerteventura to the other Canary Islands.
By sea Lanzarote: regular ferry services run from Playa Blanca to Corralejo (Fuerteventura). Fred Olsen operates the *Bocayna Express* catamaran (tel: 902 10 01 07; www.fredolsen.es); Naviera Armas operates the *Volcán de Tindaya* (tel: 928 82 49 30; www.navieraarmas.com); and Princesa Ico/Motobarcos Arosa operates the *Fuerteventura Express*

between Puerto del Carmen and Corralejo (tel: 928 51 43 22; www.princesaico.com). Naviera Aramas (► opposite) operates between Playa Blanca and Corralejo on Fuerteventura (tel: 928 85 15 42). It also has services to Gran Canaria, La Palma and Tenerife. Trasmediterránea (tel: 928 81 10 09; www.trasmediterranea.es) sails between Arrecife and Las Palmas (Gran Canaria). Líneas Marítimas Romero operates from Orzola to La Graciosa (tel: 928 84 20 55; www.lineas-romero.com).

Fuerteventura: there are regular ferry services from Morro Jable to Gran Canaria and Tenerife, a jetfoil service to Gran Canaria and ferries and high-speed catamaran services from Corralejo to Lanzarote. Trasmediterránea and Naviera Armas (tel: 928 85 08 77; www.navieraarmas.com) operate from Puerto del Rosario to Las Palmas on Gran Canaria. Naviera Armas also operates services from Morro Jable to Tenerife and from Corralejo to Playa Blanca on Lanzarote.

Getting around

PUBLIC TRANSPORT

Internal flights Daily flights between Arrecife (Lanzarote) and Puerto del Rosario (Fuerteventura) take one hour and 50 minutes and are operated by Binter Canarias (tel: 902 39 13 92; www.binternet.com).

Buses Public transport on the islands is confined mainly to a slow rural bus network designed to get villagers to and from the capital (Arrecife in Lanzarote, Puerto del Rosario in Fuerteventura), but there is a fast, frequent service between Lanzarote's resorts.

Buses are usually called by their local colloquial name, *guaguas*. Main bus station at Arrecife, Lanzarote: tel: 928 81 15 22; www.arrecifebus.com; main bus station at Puerto del Rosario, Fuerteventura: tel: 928 85 21 66; www.tiadhe.com.

Ferries For ferries that run between Lanzarote and Fuerteventura, and also to other Canary Islands (➤ 26–27).

To Isla de Lobos: Ferries Majorero, tel: 928 86 62 38, Isla de Lobos (no phone) and Celia Cruz, tel: 646 53 10 68 from Corralejo harbour, Fuerteventura.

To Isla Graciosa: Ferry Líneas Marítimas Romero from Orzola harbour, Lanzarote (tel: 928 84 20 55; www.lineas-romero.com).

TAXIS

Taxis have a green 'for hire' light inside the windscreen, and a special SP licence plate *(servicio público)*. Cab rides tend to be more expensive on Fuerteventura because distances are longer.

DRIVING

- Drive on the right.
- There are no motorways on the islands. The speed limit on main roads is 100kph (62mph) and in town is 40kph (25mph) unless indicated. Some attractions and beaches are found at the end of dirt roads.

- Seat belts are compulsory for all passengers. Children under 12 (excluding babies in rear-facing baby seats) must sit in the back.
- Driving under the influence of alcohol is strictly illegal and penalties are severe.
- Fuel is sold as *sin plomo* (unleaded) and *gasolio* (diesel). Petrol stations are rare on both islands outside the capitals and the main resorts. In the interior, some garages don't take credit cards.
- If you are involved in a serious accident, call the emergency services on 112. If no one is injured, exchange details with other motorists involved. In the event of a breakdown in a rental car, contact the emergency number supplied by the rental company.

CAR RENTAL

Car rental is relatively inexpensive on Lanzarote, but dearer on Fuerteventura. Small local firms are efficient, though the (pricier) international firms are also represented. Minor roads on both islands are often little more than dirt tracks (make sure you are covered) and signposting is sporadic.

TICKETS AND CONCESSIONS

Tickets for tourist attractions can be bought at the entrance on arrival if you are travelling independently; discounts for children and families are sometimes offered. Tickets for bus tours can be purchased at hotel receptions or from travel agents and usually include the cost of any attractions visited.

Some companies offer discounts for booking online; www.submarinesafaris.com gives 15 per cent off if tickets are bought 48 hours in advance.

Both islands are popular destinations with older travellers and senior citizen discounts are sometimes available.

Being there

TOURIST OFFICES IN LANZAROTE
Head office
● Patronato de Turismo,
Blas Cabrera Felipe,
35500 Arrecife
☎ 928 81 17 62;
www.turismolanzarote.com

Local offices
● Arrecife, Airport ☎ 928 82 07 74
● Muelle de los Mármoles
☎ 928 80 13 26
● Puerto del Carmen: in a
distinctive beachside chalet beside
the main beach, on Avenida de las
Playas ☎ 928 51 53 37
● Playa Blanca: Calle Varadero
☎ 928 51 90 18
● Costa Teguise: CC Los Charcos,
Avenida Islas Canarias
☎ 928 82 71 30
● San Bartolomé: Dr Cerdeña
Bethancourt 17 ☎ 928 52 23 51

TOURIST OFFICES IN FUERTEVENTURA
Head office
● Patronato de Turismo de
Fuerteventura,
Calle Almirante Lallermand 1,
Puerto del Rosario
☎ 928 53 08 44;
www.fuerteventuraturismo.com

Local offices
● Puerto del Rosario airport
☎ 928 86 06 04
● Corralejo: La Oliva, Plaza Pública
☎ 928 86 62 35
● Muelle de Corralejo
☎ 928 53 71 83
● Caleta de Fuste: CC Castillo
Centro ☎ 928 16 32 86
● Morro Jable: CC Shopping
Centre, Jandía Beach
☎ 928 54 07 76
● Pájara ☎ 928 54 07 76
● Betancuria ☎ 928 87 80 92

TIPS/GRATUITIES

Yes ✓   No ✗

Restaurants (service included)	✗	
Cafés/bars	✓	nearest 50 cents
Taxis	✗	
Cloakroom/washroom attendants	✓	a few cents
Tour guide	✓	€2
Room service	✓	€1
Maid service; weekly	✓	€5

CURRENCY AND FOREIGN EXCHANGE

The euro (€) is the official currency of Spain and the Canary Islands. There are banknotes for 5, 10, 20, 50, 100, 200 and 500 euros, and coins for 1, 2, 5, 10, 20 and 50 cents, and 1 and 2 euros. Banks generally offer the best rates for changing foreign currency and traveller's cheques. When changing traveller's cheques you will need to show your passport. You can also withdraw cash from ATM (cashpoint) machines.

POSTAL AND INTERNET SERVICES

Post boxes are yellow, and often have a slot marked *Extranjeros* for mail to foreign countries. Post offices are open Mon–Fri 9–2, Sat 9–1; many larger hotel receptions and shops sell stamps.

Most larger hotels on both islands have internet access; there may be a small charge. Internet cafés can be found in the main resorts, with the majority in Puerto del Carmen (Lanzarote) and Corralejo (Fuerteventura).

TELEPHONES

All phone numbers in Spain, including the Canary Islands, have 9 digits, and you must dial the whole number. To use a public payphone, you'll usually need a *tarjeta de teléfono* (phone card), available from tobacconists *(estancos)*. To dial abroad first dial 00 and the international code of the country you are calling (see below).

International dialling codes

UK: 44	Netherlands: 31
Germany: 49	Mainland Spain: 9-digit number
USA and Canada: 1	

Emergency telephone numbers

Police: 112	Ambulance: 112
Fire: 112	

EMBASSIES AND CONSULATES

UK: Las Palmas, Gran Canaria ☎ 928 26 25 08	USA: Las Palmas, Gran Canaria ☎ 928 27 12 59
Germany: Las Palmas, Gran Canaria ☎ 928 49 18 80	Netherlands: Las Palmas, Gran Canaria ☎ 928 36 22 51

HEALTH AND SAFETY

Sun advice Use a higher factor sun cream than normal, at least until your skin has begun to tan. A wide-brimmed hat and a T-shirt (even when swimming) are advisable for children.

Medication Essential medicines should be taken with you. Most well-known proprietory brands of analgesics and popular remedies are available at pharmacies. All medicines must be paid for.

Safe water Tap water is safe all over the islands, except where otherwise indicated. However most water is desalinated and tastes unpleasant. Drink bottled water *(agua mineral)*, *sin gas* (still) or *con gas* (carbonated).

Petty crime Crime is generally not a problem. Put all belongings in the boot of your car where they cannot be seen, rather than on the back seat.

● Do not leave possessions unattended on the beach.

● **In an emergency, call 112.** Otherwise call the Guardia Civil (Arrecife, tel: 928 59 21 00; Puerto del Rosario, tel: 928 85 05 03).

ELECTRICITY

The voltage is 220/240v throughout both islands. Sockets take the standard European two-round-pin plugs. Bring an adaptor for British or American appliances; change the voltage setting on US appliances.

OPENING HOURS

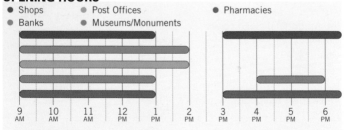

In resorts, some shops keep longer hours and may also be open on Sundays. Pharmacies keep similar hours to other shops but are usually closed on Saturday afternoons. At least one pharmacy is normally open after hours. Many bars open around 7am and stay open till about 1am or later. Museum opening times can be unpredictable – many open in the mornings only.

LANGUAGE

It is helpful to know some basic Spanish. Pronunciation guide: *b* almost like a *v*; *c* before *e* or *i* sounds like *th* otherwise like *k*; *d* like English *d* or *th*; *g* before *e* or *i* is a guttural *h*, between vowels like *h*, otherwise like *g*; *h* always silent; *j* guttural *h*; *ll* like English *lli* (as in 'million'); *ñ* sounds like *ni* in 'onion'; *qu* sound like *k*; *v* sounds a little like *b*; *z* like English *th*.

yes/no	*si/no*	I don't speak	*No hablo*
please/thank you	*por favor/gracias*	Spanish	*español*
hello/hi/good day	*hola/buenos dias*	I am .../I have ..	*Soy .../Tengo ...*
sorry, pardon me	*perdon*	help!	*socorro!*
bye, see you	*hasta luego*	how much	*cuánto es?*
that's fine	*está bien*	open/closed	*abierto/cerrado*
what?	*como?*	the toilet	*los servicios*
hotel	*hotel*	reservation	*una reserva*
room	*una habitación*	rate	*la tarifa*
single/double/twin	*individual/doble/*	breakfast	*el desayuno*
	con dos camas	bathroom	*el cuarto de baño*
one/two nights	*una noche/dos*	shower	*la ducha*
	noches	key	*la llave*
bureau de change	*cambio*	pounds sterling	*la libra esterlina*
post office	*correos*	banknote	*un billete de banco*
cash machine/ATM	*cajero automático*	travellers' cheques	*cheques de viaje*
foreign exchange	*cambio (de divisas)*	credit card	*tarjeta de crédito*
restaurant/cafe-bar	*restaurante/bar*	dessert	*el postre*
table/menu	*una mesa/la carta*	water/beer	*agua/cerveza*
today's set menu	*el plato del día*	(house) wine	*vino (de la casa)*
wine list	*la carta de vinos*	bill	*la cuenta*
plane	*el avion*	ticket	*un billete*
airport	*el aeropuerto*	single/return...	*de ida / ...de ida y*
bus	*el autobús*		*vuelta*
	('guagua')	timetable	*el horario*
ferry/terminal	*el ferry/terminus*	seat	*un asiento*

Best places to see

1 Castillo de San José

An important collection of modern art is housed in this little semicircular stone fortress on a clifftop overlooking the sea.

The commanding position of San José Castle once made it a vital defence against pirates for the island's capital and port. Today it looks down on the busy commercial harbour of Puerto de Naos.

Built of black basalt in the middle of a period of great suffering after the eruption of Timanfaya, the castle came to be known as the Hunger Fortress. It is entered by crossing a moat, and the year of its completion, 1779, is carved above the entrance. The two-storey castle possesses great elegance and charm both inside and out. Its spacious halls and spiral stairwells, and the sharp contrast of black stone and white walls, create an atmosphere of powerful, stark simplicity. Floors are paved with patterned black volcanic slabs and black pebbles. The barrel-vaulted ceilings, too, are black.

In 1976 César Manrique restored the castle and installed the Museo Internacional de Arte Contemporáneo (MIAC/International Museum of Contemporary Art) devoted to abstract modern art. The fantastic juxtaposition of vivid 20th-century forms and the black 18th-century fortress is startling. The small collection comprises sculptures and paintings by significant international and Canarian artists.

Spiral steps lead down to César Manrique's own contribution, a glass-walled restaurant and bar overlooking the sea, with black tables and chairs and modern classical music playing (► 76).

✚ 7D ✉ Carretera de Puerto de Naos, 3km (2 miles) north of Arrecife on Muelle de los Mármoles road ☎ 928 81 23 21 ❸ Museum: daily 11–9; Castle: daily 11am–midnight ✋ Inexpensive 🍴 Restaurant (€€), bar (€) 🚌 Every 30 mins from Arrecife waterfront, every hour at weekends and festivals

ℹ Blas Cabrera Felipe (by waterfront), Arrecife ☎ 928 81 17 62; www.turismolanzarote.com

2 Cueva de los Verdes (Green's Cave)

The guided 2km (1-mile) walk through part of one of the longest lava cave systems in the world is enhanced by lighting, music and natural illusions.

Monte Corona is an extinct volcano in northern Lanzarote, whose eruptions some 5,000 years ago created a *malpaís* – a contorted, blackened landscape similar to Timanfaya at the other end of the island. The Corona eruptions formed one of the world's longest lava caves, Cueva de los Verdes and neighbouring Jameos del Agua being part of the same 7.5km (4.5-mile) Corona system (of which 1.5km/1 mile is beneath the sea-bed). These hollow tubes were carved out as older basalt rock was melted and washed away by the lava flowing around it, and underground gases inflated the molten terrain.

The network of caverns and tunnels has long been known to locals, who used to hide here in the 17th century when slave hunters and pirates raided the island. Cueva de los Verdes (Verde was the family name of former owners) is a short section reached by descending to a tunnel below ground level. Hour-long guided visits in English take visitors along a circular 1km (0.5-mile) walkway, narrow and low-ceilinged in places. Haunting music and lighting heighten the experience, which takes in vividly coloured rocks, impressive rock formations and a clever optical illusion at the end of the tour.

The entrance and ticket booth to the caves have been cleverly arranged to avoid disfiguring the barren seashore *malpaís*, which can be explored on footpaths.

✚ 11E ✉ 2km (1 mile) from Arrieta (26km/16 miles north of Arrecife) ☎ 928 84 84 84 🕔 Daily 10–6 (last tour at 5) 👋 Moderate 🍴 El Charcón fish restaurant (€; ➤ 101) on Arrieta waterfront 🚌 No 9 passes about 1km (0.5 miles) away; 3 times a day Mon–Fri, twice Sat–Sun
ℹ Blas Cabrera Felipe (by waterfront), Arrecife ☎ 928 81 17 62

3 Dunes of Fuerteventura

The sun-dried, windswept island has immense beaches and tranquil, empty regions of fabulous sand dunes.

Like a miniature Sahara, the island of Fuerteventura is sandy and waterless, windy and parched. For millennia sands have blown here across the 96km (60 miles) from Africa, covering the volcanic

layer beneath, creating endless dune landscapes and great hills of pale sand.

Right behind Fuerteventura's main resort, Corralejo, on the island's northern tip, rises its largest and most impressive single area of dunes. This complex system of dazzling pale sands, stretching about 10km (6 miles) along the coast and reaching 2–3km (1–2 miles) inland from the shore, has been declared a protected zone known as the Parque Natural de las Dunas de Corralejo.

Fuerteventura has another major dune area at the Istmo de la Pared, the narrow isthmus of mountainous dunes separating Jandía Peninsula from the rest of the island. Much of the peninsula is now protected as a Natural Park. At some stage in prehistory, the dunes did not exist and Jandía was a separate volcanic island.

Fuerteventura's dunes are neither barren nor lifeless. As well as forming spectacular beaches, they also support unusual plant species that can thrive in these dry, salty sands. Some are found only here, including a yellow-flowering shrub, *Lotus lancerottense*, *Echium handiense* with its bluebell flowers, and a red-flowered succulent, *Euphorbia handiensis*.

➕ 18H (Dunas de Corralejo) and 18R (Istmo de la Pared)
🍴 Restaurants (€–€€) on seafront in Corralejo. Also El Camello (€–€€) at La Pared 🚌 No 6 (Corralejo–Puerto del Rosario) hourly 🚢 Corralejo–Playa Blanca on Lanzarote takes 20 mins
ℹ Plaza Pública, Corralejo ☎ 928 86 62 35; CC Shopping Centre, Morro Jable ☎ 928 54 07 76;
www.fuerteventuraturismo.com

4 Fundación César Manrique

César Manrique's own home, half submerged in a string of volcanic bubbles in the rock, displays to the full his tremendous artistic flair.

Manrique (1919–92) had a special interest in mobiles and one extraordinary example is the huge complex of colour and movement standing at the entrance to his own home. It is best seen at night, when the mobile and the house are not so much illuminated as dotted with light.

Here architecture is fun, astonishing and brilliant. The visible exterior of the building, inspired by traditional local style, combines dazzling white with jet black. Around it, a garden of cacti, succulents and semicircles of stone is set between white and black walls. Immense cylindrical cacti look like green Doric columns. Above the doorway, note Manrique's 'logo' – an interlocked C and M said to resemble a devil.

Since Manrique's death, the interior has become an art gallery, made up mainly of his private collection. It includes works by most of the big names of 20th-century abstract and modern art, including Tapiès, Miró and Picasso, as well as a number of Manrique's own powerful canvases.

Steps lead down into five volcanic bubbles (created during the eruptions of 1730–36), each made into a complete room with distinctive character, colour and furniture. One has a trickling fountain, another a palm tree growing up through the roof. The dining room has an open grill, a pool

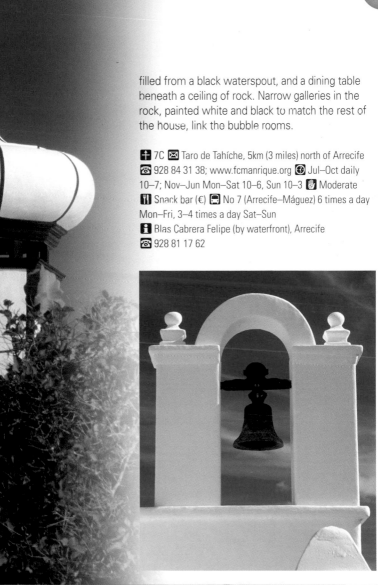

filled from a black waterspout, and a dining table beneath a ceiling of rock. Narrow galleries in the rock, painted white and black to match the rest of the house, link the bubble rooms.

🕆 7C ✉ Taro de Tahíche, 5km (3 miles) north of Arrecife
☎ 928 84 31 38; www.fcmanrique.org 🕒 Jul–Oct daily 10–7; Nov–Jun Mon–Sat 10–6, Sun 10–3 ✋ Moderate
🍴 Snack bar (€) 🚌 No 7 (Arrecife–Máguez) 6 times a day Mon–Fri, 3–4 times a day Sat–Sun
ℹ Blas Cabrera Felipe (by waterfront), Arrecife
☎ 928 81 17 62

5 Islote de Hilario (Timanfaya)

The heart and soul of Lanzarote is an awesome red and black volcano called Islote de Hilario, or Fire Mountain.

Lanzarote's main Fire Mountain is sleeping – for the moment. Visible from afar, the volcano dominates the view and the thoughts of visitors and locals alike. Its catastrophic force once destroyed in an instant the livelihood of most of the islanders, yet it is now Lanzarote's most spectacular attraction. Of the several volcanic points on the island, including the other mountains of fire within the Timanfaya National Park (► 130–135), this is the most ferocious.

The sculpted landscape all around leaves no doubt that this is a volcano with a temper. Here and there tortured rocks are streaked with colour, where stones have fused in the heat. The *malpaís* (badlands) around the mountain show not a blade of grass, but do support lichen and small plants.

The usual way to reach Islote de Hilario's summit is to drive along a roadway, where the lingering volcanic heat remains hottest. At the very top, a big, convivial restaurant called El Diablo (The Devil) is an incongruous oasis of life amid the arid wilderness. Conceived and constructed by César Manrique, the restaurant is a glass-walled circle giving panoramic views of the volcanic terrain and the sea beyond. Waiters serve delicious volcano-cooked marinated pork, seared chicken and fresh fish at this unique barbecue, accompanied by salty *papas arrugadas* and local wines.

By the entrance to El Diablo take a look at the wide opening resembling a well. This 'well' descends into fiery earth, not water, and the restaurant's meat and fish are cooked in the oven-like 300°C (570°F) heat that wafts up from the volcano. At other places close by, the surface of the ground is too hot to walk on, sometimes reaching a blistering 100°C (212°F). The temperature just 13m (43ft) underground reaches 600°C (1,110°F).

Outside the restaurant, park staff make the volcano do impressive tricks for tourists: a bunch of brushwood thrown into a hollow quickly bursts into flames; a bucket of water emptied into a hole roars straight back as an immense spout of steam. In front of the restaurant buses set off on the round tour of the park included in the entrance fee.

When Timanfaya erupted in 1730, it threw a thick layer of burning rocks over the cornfields of western Lanzarote. During the six years that the eruption continued, the fertile western end of the island was devastated, and several villages in the Timanfaya area were destroyed. Today life has returned to normal at villages where the lava flow stopped and the grey-black pebbles of volcanic debris *(picón)* have been found to aid agriculture, and are now being sold to farmers on other islands.

➕ 3C ✉ Timanfaya National Park, 7km (4 miles) north of Yaiza ☎ 928 84 00 57 🕐 Daily 9–6 ✋ Moderate (includes bus tour) 🍴 El Diablo (€€) restaurant (12–3:30) and snack bar (9am–4:45) 🚫 None, but coaches leave from resorts ❓ The last Volcano Route bus tour leaves at 5pm. Extensive free car-parking facilities at the summit ℹ Avenida de las Playas, Puerto del Carmen ☎ 928 51 33 51

6 Jameos del Agua

**César Manrique turned this bizarre
volcanic feature into one of the island's
most intriguing sights, an exotic
subterranean water garden.**

A *jameo* is an underground volcanic tunnel whose
roof has partly collapsed. Until Manrique set to
work, this one was just a hole in the ground.

Jameos del Agua is reached from the surface by
wooden spiral stairs that twist down into the earth.
At the bottom, astonishingly, a restaurant and
dance floor look over an eerie underground lake;
tiny, blind white crabs live in its perfectly
transparent water. At the lake's far end, the arty
tables of another bar perch on little terraces where
you can sit with a meal or a drink.

This mysterious environment, within a roof-
less cavern below sea-level, is truly hard to
comprehend at first. Whatever the weather
outside, here the air is still and balmy, and full
of the songs of tiny birds.

From the bar, meandering paths lead upwards
among rocks and plant beds to a dazzling man-
made blue and white pool. More spiral steps wind
steeply up to the edges of the *jameos*, giving
thrilling views down into this extraordinary meeting
point of man and nature.

At the top is the Casa de los Volcanes (House of
Volcanoes), a science museum devoted mainly to
volcanic activity.

On Tuesday, Friday and Saturday evenings,
Jameos del Agua turns into a spectacular
subterranean nightclub.

🕀 11E 🖂 2km (1 mile) from Arrieta, 26km (16 miles) north
of Arrecife ☎ 928 84 80 20 🕐 Daily 10–6:30; also Tue, Fri,
Sat 7:30pm–2am (folklore show 11pm) ✋ Moderate
🍴 Restaurant (€€, evenings only), two snack bars (€, all
day) 🚌 No 9 (Arrecife–Orzola) several times a day
ℹ Blas Cabrera Felipe (by waterfront), Arrecife
☎ 928 81 17 62

7 Jardín de Cactus (Cactus Garden)

Manrique transformed a disused quarry into this extraordinary formal garden with over 1,400 varieties of cactus.

The fields of cactus around Guatiza and Mala, north of Arrecife, used to be cultivated to provide a home to the cochineal beetle, whose larvae provides a bright red dye. Now the most striking landmark in the cactus district is César Manrique's towering 8m (26ft) green metal cactus outside the entrance to his Cactus Garden.

Formerly a hand-dug quarry, the garden is an oval-shaped enclosure descending in narrow concentric stone terraces. Each terrace is now covered with *picón* (porous volcanic granules). Growing from the black ash like bizarre artworks are 1,420 species of cactus, a total of almost 10,000 plants, each standing separate from the rest and demanding attention.

Some are like porcupines, some like wedding cakes covered in hair, some like prickly rockets, some spreading themselves like octopuses, others uncoiling like snakes. Others seem to have come straight out of a Wild West cartoon strip. Many have florid, gaudy blooms, others tiny, delicate flowers, sometimes strung around the plant.

Visitors walk carefully around the terraces, gradually descending to a lower central area, where there is a miniature water garden and remnants of the quarry. A terrace rather wider than the rest

accommodates a stylish bar, where circular wooden tables under pale sailcloth awnings offer a view of the entire garden.

Behind the bar, an old windmill rises above the garden and the surrounding landscape. Beautifully restored, it is sadly no longer used for grinding grain.

✚ 8B ✉ Guatiza (17 km/10.5 miles northeast of Arrecife)
☎ 928 52 93 97 🕓 Daily 10–5:45 ✋ Moderate; includes free drink 🍴 Bar/café (€) 🚌 None Tour buses make daily trips
ℹ Blas Cabrera Felipe (by waterfront), Arrecife
☎ 928 81 17 62

8 Mirador del Río

A touch of Manrique magic has made a clifftop view of little Isla Graciosa into one of the loveliest places on the island.

A *mirador* is a viewpoint, and El Río, literally 'the river', is the name of the narrow strait between Lanzarote and its little sister island, La Graciosa. Outside the Mirador, one of Manrique's open metalwork signs stands in front of a daunting stone wall that actually conceals the view, with just a porthole hinting at what lies on the other side. Before César Manrique set to work, Bateria del Río, an old artillery post, perched here, 480m (1,575ft) high on the Famara cliffs with a commanding view

over La Graciosa and the islands of Montaña Clara and Alegranza beyond.

Manrique's first thought was to create a restaurant here. He had a large room chipped out of the clifftop, and roofed it with two domes covered with earth and grass. It is entered through a long, winding white tunnel and spiral staircase, which plays with brilliant effect on the themes of light, space and air.

The white room – or rooms, for the domes break up the space – is exquisite, its simplicity, clarity and spaciousness a delight to the eye. Neat wooden tables provide a place to sit and relax, and a most unusual-looking bar serves drinks and snacks. There is also a balcony, where you can stand in the open air by a sheer drop.

The main attraction, however, is the view itself, a spectacular vista of sea and sky, in which La Graciosa floats as if itself suspended like a sculpture.

➕ 11D ✉ 7km (23 miles) north of Haría ☎ 928 52 65 48 🕐 Daily 10–5:45 💶 Inexpensive 🍴 Bar/café (€) 🚌 None, but tour buses from resorts 🛳 To visit La Graciosa, catch a ferry from nearby Orzola

ℹ Blas Cabrera Felipe (by waterfront), Arrecife ☎ 928 81 17 62

Teguise

9

Lanzarote's former capital is today barely more than a village, but it still has the island's most elegant buildings and greatest charm.

Until 1852 this tiny town was Lanzarote's capital, in the centre of the island, out of reach of the coast's raiders and pirates. Founded in the 15th century by Maciot de Béthencourt, nephew of Lanzarote's Norman conqueror Jean de Béthencourt, it stands on the native islanders' ancient meeting point, known as Acatife. Locals still regard this as the island's real capital, while Arrecife remains *el puerto*, the port.

Teguise has an Iberian colonial style with a handsome square, a grid of narrow cobbled streets and a church. For 100 years it remained the Canaries' most important town, home of European nobility – the de Béthencourts, the Herreras and others – and gave birth to much Canarian folk culture, including its unique instrument, the *timple*.

Many buildings here still possess a certain splendour. In the main square is the white-capped landmark church, Iglesia de Nuestra Señora de Guadalupe (also known as San Miguel), and the

Renaissance mansion Palacio de Spinola (or Espiñola), former home of an 18th-century Genoese merchant, now a museum. The savings bank Caja de Canarios occupies a 15th-century tithe barn.

In the charming, smaller Plaza del 18 de Julio, the old hospital dates from 1473, and the snow-white, balconied Casa Cuartel, once an army barracks, from the 17th century. The two conventual churches, the Franciscans' 16th-century San Francisco and Dominicans' 17th-century San Domingo, are a short walk away.

Thousands of people arrive every Sunday for the morning market, one of the Canaries' largest.

✚ 7B ✉ 9km (5.5 miles) north of Arrecife 🍴 Ikarus (€€€), Plaza del 18 de Julio 🚌 No 6 (Arrecife–Playa Blanca) one bus each way Sun only. No 7, 6 times a day Mon–Fri, 3–4 times Sat–Sun. No 9 (Arrecife–Orzola) several times a day. Nos 11 and 12 twice a day Sun only from Costa Teguise and Puerto del Carmen. Most tour operators run coach trips to market on Sunday

❓ Local festivals: Cabalgata de los Reyes Magos, 5 Jan; Teguise Carnival, Feb or Mar; Fiesta de Nuestra Señora del Carmen, 16 Jul

ℹ️ San Bartolomé: Dr Cerdeña Bethancourt 17 ☎ 928 52 23 51; www.teguise.com

10 Valle de la Geria

The extraordinary vineyards in this blackened landscape within the protected area of La Geria make a dramatic backdrop to fascinating wine shops and museums.

It might seem unlikely that a blasted rocky terrain covered with grey volcanic debris would be among the most intriguing and even beautiful of landscapes. In places the ground has been shattered by volcanic activity, sliced and patterned by deep narrow fissures. Far beneath the solid surface, molten lava is still moving.

If you look carefully, you will see that this land is full of life: tiny white and coloured living specks dot the dark volcanic stones – these are minuscule lichens and tiny succulents; unexpected dips and hollows harbour little clusters of lush natural greenery; and in spring, the roadsides are lined with wild flowers, some strikingly coloured, like the purple poppies.

Most remarkable are the vineyards, each vine growing deep in a separate hollow dug into the shingly rock. Each hollow shelters behind its own semicircular rock wall. This gives the vines just enough shade and protection to survive, and catch what little moisture can be gathered through

ARTESANIA

dew and condensation. So successful is the method, which has to be done completely by hand, that it produces high yields of grapes. Though cleverly functional, the rows of little horseshoe walls look more like art than agriculture: César Manrique's 'landscape as art' has here become 'farming as geometry'. The majority of vines produce Malvasia grapes, and the wine they make – fresh, somewhat sweet whites – can be tasted and bought at the various *bodegas* (wine cellars) off the Uga–Masdache road and in Uga itself.

When stopping to explore, remember that the cutting edges of the rough, sharp, brittle black rocks and stones make walking difficult and unpleasant, and can destroy a pair of shoes in minutes.

✚ 4D ✉ East of Uga; along the Uga–Masdache road (LZ30) 🚌 None
❓ Wine-growers' *bodegas* such as El Grifo (☎ 928 52 49 51; www.elgrifo.com) and La Geria (☎ 928 17 31 78) offer wine-tasting. El Grifo also has an interesting wine museum
🛈 Avenida de las Playas, Puerto del Carmen ☎ 928 51 33 51

Best things to do

Best spas

LANZAROTE
Aquarsis Thermal Spa and Wellness Centre
Book a massage or algae wrap at this intimate centre, then relax in the hydrotherapy pool, followed by a sauna or Turkish bath.

✉ Calle Chalana 1, Puerto del Carmen ☎ 928 51 13 37; www.aquarsis.es

Hesperia Lanzarote
This decadent, Balinese-style spa has a full range of beauty treatments and packages from one to six days.

✉ Hesperia Hotel, Puerto Calero ☎ 828 08 08 20;
www.hesperia-lanzarote.com

Hotel Beatriz Spa
This Roman-style spa is one of the best on the island, featuring ice baths, jacuzzis and tepidariums, plus a full range of treatments.

✉ Calle Atalaya s/n, Costa Teguise ☎ 928 59 08 28;
www.beatrizhoteles.com

Meliá Volcán
Underwater jet streams are just part of the 'Thermal Universe' here, which includes a Cleopatra day package – be queen for a day. Turkish bath, Finnish sauna and Scottish showers too.

✉ Castillo del Águila ☎ 928 51 91 85; www.solmelia.com

Thalasso Rubicón
A slick health and beauty centre with hydrotherapy pool and beds, power jet treatments, jacuzzis, saunas and Turkish baths.

✉ Montaña Roja, Playa Blanca ☎ 928 51 85 00; www.h10hotels.com

Thalassotherapy Centre
The latest addition to Lanzarote's spa scene offers massages with detoxifying Atlantic sea salt, some excellent, reasonably priced packages and a garden lounge area.

✉ Hotel Iberostar, Puerto Calero ☎ 928 84 95 95; www.iberostar.com

FUERTEVENTURA
Barceló Fuerteventura Thalasso Spa
This is a modern thalassotherapy centre, with a sauna and Turkish bath in a four-star hotel.
✉ Caleta de Fuste ☎ 928 54 75 17; www.barcelo.com

Gran Hotel Atlantis Bahía Real
Luxurious treatments – both medicinal and beautifying – make use of local, natural resources, such as salt water and hot stones.
✉ Avenida Grandes Playas s/n, Corralejo ☎ 928 53 64 44;
www.atlantishotels.com

Hesperides Spa Thalasso
Rejuvenation is key at this spacious spa, with a very full range of facilities from Niagara baths to an ice igloo.
✉ Carretera FV-2 KM 11 ☎ 928 49 51 00; www.starwoodhotels.com

Suite-Hotel Atlantis
A compact spa with saunas, jacuzzi and gym offering excellent massages and beauty treatments.
✉ Calle Las Dunas, Corralejo ☎ 928 53 52 58; www.atlantishotels.com

BEST THINGS TO DO

Good places to have lunch

LANZAROTE
Bodega El Chupadero (€€)
This little gem, tucked away in the heart of the vineyards of La Geria, is a perfect stop on a wine tour. Enjoy delicious tapas on the terrace of this *bodega* (closed Mon).

✉ Signposted off the LZ30, opposite the Ermita La Geria, La Asomada
☎ 928 17 31 15; www.el-chupadero.com

Casal Cura (€€)
In the north of the island, this is one of Lanzarote's best restaurants. Several local stews like *sancocho*, *puchero* and *potaje* (➤ 14) are served in small intimate dining rooms.

✉ Calle Nueva 1, Haría ☎ 928 83 55 56

El Diablo (€€)
El Diablo has wonderful panoramic views, and traditional Canarian cuisine cooked over heat rising directly from the earth (➤ 44–45).

✉ Islote de Hilario, Parque Nacional de Timanfaya ☎ 928 84 00 57

La Lonja (€–€€)

In the middle of Puerto del Carmen's Old Port, this unpretentious restaurant is a busy quayside spot packed with locals, serving fresh fish and lobster.

✉ Calle Varadero, Puerto del Carmen ☎ 928 51 13 77

Mesón La Jordana (€€€)

One of Lanzarote's top restaurants, with country-style decor and an imaginative menu that includes wild boar and garlic prawns (closed Sun).

✉ Calle Los Geranios, Costa Teguise ☎ 928 59 03 28

Punta Fariones (€–€€)

Sample some good-value seafood at this simple restaurant by Orzola's little harbour.

✉ Calle La Quemadita, Orzola ☎ 928 84 25 58

FUERTEVENTURA

Casa Santa María (€€–€€€)

This bar-restaurant, in a rustic 16th-century house, offers some of the best Canarian cooking on Fuerteventura. Enjoy the lovely views and watch local artists and craftspeople at work.

✉ Plaza Santa María de Betancuria 1, Betancuria ☎ 928 87 80 36

La Marquesina (€€)

Watch the world go by at this relaxed and unpretentious place at the harbour, popular with locals. Fresh fish a speciality.

✉ Muelle Chico, Corralejo ☎ 928 53 54 35

La Vaca Azul (€€)

Enjoy unspoilt sea views from this lovely beachside restaurant. Despite the name – The Blue Cow – it specializes in fish. Consider visiting at sunset for a great view from the terrace (closed Tue).

✉ Old harbour, El Cotillo ☎ 928 53 86 85

Top activities

Cycling: Thanks to the dry weather and lack of traffic, cycle touring is fun on these islands. Choose between easy-going flatter terrain near the resorts, and more challenging hills inland. Wherever you go take plenty of drinking water.

Deep-sea fishing: Hunting for bluefin, barracuda, swordfish, marlin, tuna, dorado and the other big Atlantic fish is popular on both islands. Rent a boat or join an excursion.

Diving and scuba diving: Good underwater visibility in a climate where diving is possible year-round, has made this a favourite sport on the two islands. The underwater lava has created many reefs, caves and unusual rock formations. There is an abundance of wildlife to be seen, including sharks, eels, octopus and rays, as well as sponges, anenomes, crustaceans and colourful coral.

Golf: Dramatic landscapes, lush grass and good weather year round mean it is easy to get into full swing on either of the islands. Eighteen-hole courses can be found at Costa Teguise, Lanzarote and Fuerteventura's Las Playitas and Caleta de Fuste. Several new courses on both islands are being built, but progress is slow.

Paragliding, hang-gliding, skyjumping: These are all keenly practised on Lanzarote – by experts. Unpredictable winds (strong at higher altitudes) increase the thrill for the most experienced, but make the sports off-limits for beginners. The most popular spots, especially for hang-gliders, are the soaring sea cliffs at Famara in the north of the island. It's best to bring your own equipment.

Surfing: Warm waters, high winds (particularly in winter) and almost constant sunshine make surfing on both islands popular with experts and beginners. The heavily indented coastline offers a wide variety of breaks, with Famara on Lanzarote one of the best spots. Instructors and boards can be hired.

Walking: There are numerous possible routes on both islands, but note that walking on the volcanic *malpaís* is difficult and uncomfortable. Don't set off on your own, and take adequate supplies (of drinking water, high-energy food and protective gear) with you on longer trips. Wear sturdy footwear. Walking on Fuerteventura's vast dunes is more like an expedition in a desert than a stroll on the beach.

Windsurfing, kitesurfing and kiteboarding: Great beaches and stiff breezes create ideal conditions, especially on the coasts of Fuerteventura's Corralejo (➤ 169) and Jandía Peninsula (➤ 172–173). Most of the main resort beaches in Lanzarote and Fuerteventura have facilities for windsurfing rentals and instruction, while many surf schools offer kitesurfing tuition. Fuerteventura is considered one of the world's best locations for windsurfing, and Jandía's Playa de Sotavento is the site of the annual World Windsurfing Championships mid-July to mid-August. It has also hosted the Kiteboard World Cup.

Best beaches

LANZAROTE
Caletón Blanco
Warm and sheltered beach 1km (0.5 miles) southeast of Orzola on Lanzarote. The swimming is safe here and there are rock pools to explore.

Playa de las Conchas
Off the coast of Lanzarote on Isla Graciosa, this beautiful, isolated, golden beach is one of the most gorgeous in the archipelago; but strong currents make it dangerous to swim here (➤ 93).

Playa Dorada
Round the corner from Playa Blanca, this delightful golden crescent in a sheltered bay is perfect for swimming and sunbathing. Dominated by the massive Hotel Princesa Yaiza and a shopping centre. Good for children.

Playa de Famara
Vast sandy beach considered one of the best on the less developed northwest coast of Lanzarote; swimming is discouraged here as the undercurrents are dangerous (➤ 89).

Playa Grande (Playa Blanca)
Lanzarote's main family beach at Puerto del Carmen is a good base for watersports. The broad pale yellow sands are always packed, lined with blue and orange umbrellas and the backdrop of the Avenida de las Playas (➤ 140).

Playa de Mujeres
Set on the southern tip of Lanzarote, this lovely beach, backed by sandy cliffs, is one of the longest stretches in the area (➤ 126).

Playa de Papagayo
There is nowhere else on Lanzarote that is remotely as beautiful as the Papagayo sands; perfect for determined sun lovers (➤ 126).

Playa de los Pocillos
Another of Puerto del Carmen's beaches and the largest. An immense sweep of sand, popular for sunbathing and swimming (➤ 141). The Jameos end has child-friendly snackbars and restaurants.

FUERTEVENTURA
Playa de Barlovento
On the western side of the Jandía Peninsula the vast untouched golden sands are picture-postcard perfect. Never swim on the Barlovento coastline, even if the waters look calm, as there are treacherous undercurrents (➤ 173).

Playas de Corralejo
The family resort of Corralejo has glorious soft sands stretching for around 10km (6 miles), backed by huge dunes where you can wander out of sight and away from any distractions, apart from a nudist here and there (➤ 169).

Playa de Sotavento
On the southeast-facing coast of the Jandía Peninsula, this 30km-long (18-mile) expanse of sand is one of the most photgraphed beaches in the Canary Islands. It is more sheltered than many beaches on this windy island, hence its name, meaning leeward (➤ 172).

Stunning views

LANZAROTE
Castillo de Santa Bárbara
On a clear day you can see for miles looking down onto Teguise and across the island from the splendidly situated Santa Bárbara Castle (► 84–85).

Helicopter or light airplane tour
There's only one way to see the craters of Timanfaya and the Caldera Blanca, or to appreciate just why Arrecife was so named (after the offshore reefs that make it a natural harbour) – and that's from the air. A helicopter or airplane trip doesn't come cheap – either to your pocket or the environment – but for many it's a real thrill and the views are spectacular.
Helitours ✉ Lanzarote airport, Arrecife ☎ 628 13 68 24; www.helitourservice.com
Lanza Air ☎ 928 80 62 15

Mirador del Río
This is probably the most impressive *mirador* (look-out point) in the whole archipelago and offers vertiginous views of Isla Graciosa (► 50–51).

Peñas del Chache
César Manrique very much enjoyed his holidays in Famara as a child. One of his unfinished projects was a *mirador* on top of the cliffs at Peñas del Chache, looking down onto his beloved Famara.

FUERTEVENTURA
Mirador del Morro de Velosa
Just outside Betancuria on the FV30 look high above you and
you will see a large chalet-style building with picture windows.
Stop here and the admire sweeping panoramas of Betancuria
Rural Park.

Montaña La Caldera
If you are very fit, you can climb this steep 127m (416ft) volcano,
dominating the tiny Isla de Lobos just off Fuerteventura, to the
crater's edge for rewarding views of Lobos itself, Lanzarote and
Fuerteventura.

Volcán de Bayuyo
On the FV101 just outside Corralejo and rising 271m (889ft) in the
air, from the Volcán de Bayuyo you can look down into Corralejo's
'backyard' and across to Isla de Lobos and Lanzarote.

Pico de Zarza
Climb Fuerteventura's highest peak (812m/2,664ft), an extinct
volcano in Jandía Peninsula for panoramic views. It's a five-hour
hike and you will need to bring food and water.

Montaña Tindaya
On a clear day from Tindaya mountain (399m/1,309ft), there are
magnificent views of Mount Teide, Tenerife's highest peak. Ring
the Environment Department (tel: 928 86 23 63) first to obtain
permission.

a walk around Isla de Lobos

A walk around this tiny desert island makes a tranquil day trip. The nature reserve attracts walkers and bird-watchers, who come to spot petrels and osprey. Bring a picnic, water and protection from the sun, and stick to the tracks.

Catch the first ferry from Corralejo, which leaves at around 10am and takes 30 minutes. On arrival at El Puertito, head off to the right on the main wide track.

At once the track leads through rough terrain of lava and sand. The volcanic rock is streaked and coloured with little plants. On the right is the pretty, rocky Caleta de la Rasca bay, with views towards the dunes of Fuerteventura.

Follow the track through rocky and then sandier terrain. At a succession of little turnings, keep left on the track.

It takes less than an hour to reach the *faro* (lighthouse) at Punta Martiño, at the other end of the island. From here there's a great view back across Lobos and to Fuerteventura and the pale beaches on Lanzarote's southern shore. This is the place to relax with a picnic.

The track now heads towards the middle of the island, with the volcanic Montaña La Caldera rising to the right of the path. At a right turn, walk away from the main track towards the volcano – there are other tracks off to the right and left, but keep heading towards the crater.

After a few minutes' climb you reach the crater edge, from where there's a terrific view of both Fuerteventura and Lanzarote.

Back on the main track, follow it as it curves round to reach the beach near the ferry harbour. Walk on past the beach to get back to the ferry. The boat back to Corralejo leaves at 4, and arrives at about 4:35.

Distance 10km (6 miles), plus ferry ride
Time 3 hours, plus about 1 hour on the ferry
Start/end point Corralejo ✚ 17G
Lunch Picnic at the lighthouse

Best buys

African craftwork
Colourful African stalls bring an exotic note to the market squares of Lanzarote and Fuerteventura. Items for sale include carved wooden masks, wooden toys, studded or tooled leatherwork and African drums. Nothing has a marked price and watch out for fakes. Don't buy ivory goods (illegal in the EU) or cheap European and Far Eastern imitations.

Ceramics
Tiles, glazed pottery and attractively handpainted crockery make excellent gifts or souvenirs but can be heavy and fragile for air-travellers. However, small items, well packed, make a distinctive and worthwhile purchase.

Crafts
As well as fine cloth goods, you'll also see good costume jewellery (often including peridot, the translucent semiprecious volcanic stone), basketware, straw hats and unusual local pottery, traditionally made without a potter's wheel. Handicrafts with delicate woodwork include the *timple*, the tiny Canarian stringed instrument.

Food and drink
For foodies, interesting presents or tasty reminders of your stay include *mojo* sauces, available in small gift packs, and local wine, which can be chosen and sampled in *bodegas*.

Flowers that fly
Exotic, Canary-grown strelitzias – bird-of-paradise flowers – are widely available and make an impressive gift. They should be ordered in advance and picked up on the day of your departure. They come specially wrapped and packaged for air travel.

Local lace, crochet and embroidery
The most common items are table-cloths, placemats, napkins, bedlinen and handkerchiefs. They are good value for high-quality handmade work, and have distinctively Spanish designs.

Duty-free goods
The Canary Islands are exempt from certain taxes and duties on goods imported from outside the EU. In the main towns and tourist resorts, shops offer electronic goods, cameras, binoculars and other optical equipment, CD and DVD players, perfumes and other luxury items at discount prices. Prices are similar to those in airport shops and other duty-free outlets. Alcohol is especially good value. Beware though, do not simply assume 'tax-free' prices are a bargain: you can pay almost as much (and sometimes more) than the usual shop price. Be on your guard against imitations with fake designer names. Remember that bona fide electronic goods should be accompanied by proper international warranties and service details.

Manrique designs
T-shirts and other clothes with Manrique logos and designs, jewellery and decorative goods designed by him, and prints of his work are available at Fundación César Manrique shops:

✉ Casa-Museo Fundación César Manrique, Taro de Tahíche (main shop); also
✉ 26 José Betancort, Arrecife; 10 Diaz Otilía, Arrecife; Arrecife airport; La Lonja, Playa Blanca; Avenida Papagayo 6, Playa Blanca; Tourist Office, Avenida de las Playas, Puerto del Carmen; Calle Plaza del 18 de Julio 6, Teguise

Places to take the children

LANZAROTE
Aguapark
This small water park has decent waterslides and flumes, but the water isn't heated and there is little shade.

✉ 2km (1 mile) inland from Costa Teguise ☎ 928 59 21 28 🕐 Daily 10–6
✋ Expensive

Camel rides
Unlike other camel rides, the rides based at the Camel Park below Timanfaya (➤ 131) don't involve sitting on the camel, but in seats on the animal's side.

Gran Karting Club
Lanzarote's premier go-karting track. Karts come in all sizes to suit adults and children. The site also has a bar, café and playground.

✉ La Rinconada, Arrecife road, Puerto del Carmen ☎ 619 75 99 46;
www.grankarting.com 🕐 Daily 10–9 ✋ Moderate

Guinate Parque Tropical
Little ones will enjoy the exotic bird and animal shows at this tropical park (➤ 89).

✉ Guinate (4km/2.5 miles) from Haría ☎ 928 83 55 00 🕐 Daily 10–5
✋ Moderate

Jameos del Agua
See pages 46–47.

FUERTEVENTURA
Baku Water Park
As well as its water rides, the 'Baku Village' has ten-pin bowling, crazy golf, and 'Animal Experience', allowing children to get up close to – and even swim with – creatures such as sea lions.

✉ Avenida Nuestra Señora del Carmen, Corralejo ☎ 928 86 72 27;
www.bakufuerteventura.com 🕐 See website for opening times ✋ Expensive

Corralejo Carnaval

A dazzling show over two weeks that allows wild behaviour; a day is specially devoted to the children's carnival. Failing that, enjoy the crazy noise, colour and flamboyance of any local fiesta.

🕐 Feb or Mar 🖐 Free

La Lajita Oasis Park

The main attraction of this zoo is a ride on one of its herd of dromedaries. An African savannah features exotic animals. As well as various shows to watch – sea lions, birds of prey or crocodiles – there are many birds, primates, giraffes and rhinoceroses. You can buy exotic flora at the garden centre.

✉ Carretera General de Jandía, FV-2 Km 57 ☎ 928 16 11 35; www.lajitaoasispark.com 🕐 Daily 9–6 🖐 Expensive

La Rosita

This old country house is now a small farm and museum where you can take a camel ride through the hills and get up close to farm animals.

✉ Vilaverde, Carretera La Oliva–Corralejo ☎ 928 17 53 25 🕐 Mon–Sat 10–6 🖐 Moderate

Boat excursions

LANZAROTE
Catamaran
The 23m (75ft) luxury catamaran
Catlanza will transport you to the
Papagayo beaches, where jet-ski rides
and snorkelling are available. Also
operates out of Corralejo on
Fuerteventura.

✉ Puerto Calero marina, just south of Puerto
del Carmen ☎ 928 513 022;
www.catlanza.com ✋ Expensive (includes
food, drink and bus transfers)

Ferry
Take the 45-minute crossing to Fuerteventura where you will have
2 hours to explore the beaches and town of Corralejo. Your journey
continues to Isla de Lobos, where there is a chance to snorkel or
ride a banana boat.

✉ Playa Blanca ☎ 928 81 36 08; www.cesardos.com 🕓 Mon–Sat 10:15am
✋ Expensive (includes food and drink)

Fishing
Try some big-game fishing and catch a shark, swordfish or tuna, or
go 'bottom fishing' while the boat is anchored.

✉ Calle Teide 8, Puerto del Carmen ☎ 928 51 43 22; www.anasegundo.com
🕓 Mon–Sat ✋ Expensive

Submarine
Dive in a real yellow submarine up to 50m (165ft) below the
waves, with high-tech viewing. No under-2s.

✉ Puerto Calero ☎ 928 51 28 98; www.submarinesafaris.com ✋ Expensive

FUERTEVENTURA
Catamaran
Glass-bottomed catamaran boat trips to Isla de Lobos on the *Celia Cruz*.

✉ Corralejo ☎ 646 53 10 68 🌐 Daily at 9:45am, returning at 2:20pm and 5pm 💷 Moderate

Ferry
Get to Lanzarote in just 12 minutes on the *Bocayna Express*, with a bus transfer to Puerto del Carmen

✉ Corralejo ☎ 922 62 82 00; www.fredolsen.es

Oceanarium Explorer
A large family-orientated operation. Before boarding the vessel you visit an aquarium on dry land. You then set sail on either the biggest catamaran on the island or a glass-bottomed boat. Sailings last between 30 minutes and 4 hours.

✉ Caleta de Fuste ☎ 928 16 35 14 🌐 Daily 💷 Expensive

Submarine
This twin-hulled submarine will take you 30m (100ft) under the sea. Trips last 90 minutes, with 30 minutes under water.

✉ Morro Jable port ☎ 900 50 70 06; www.subcat-fuerteventura.com
💷 Expensive

Whale/dolphin watching
The *Siña María* is a luxury boat operating from Corralejo, offering excursions dedicated to spotting dolphins and whales. Trips include snorkelling and swimming off Isla de Lobos.

✉ Corralejo (kiosk on the harbour) ☎ 686 72 53 27 🌐 Tue, Thu, Sat
💷 Expensive (includes buffet lunch and drinks)

Meals with a view

LANZAROTE
Castillo de San José (€€)
Inside the Castillo, attached to the modern art museum, and facing the sea through a panoramic window, this restaurant was designed by César Manrique as a work of art itself (➤ 37). There are black walls, black tables, even black napkins, and modern classical music playing. The food is sophisticated and well presented, with a moderately priced menu of the day.

✉ Carretera de Puerto Naos (3km/2 miles north of Arrecife on Muelle de los Mármoles road) ☎ 928 81 23 21 🕓 1pm–3:45pm and 7pm–11pm. Bar 11am–1am. Can be visited without going to the museum

Jardín de Cactus (€)
Big wooden tables under a sail-cloth awning beneath the windmill. Have a drink or a light meal and gaze at Manrique's cactus collection (➤ 48–49).

✉ Jardín de Cactus, Guatiza (17km/10 miles northeast of Arrecife) ☎ 928 52 93 97 🕓 Daily 10–5:30

Panorámico Altamar (€€)
Eating here is like dining in a glass box, 17 storeys looking out over the capital. The menu features innovative international and Mediterranean dishes. It's not cheap, but when you consider the exceptional surroundings, it's very reasonable.

✉ Arrecife Gran Hotel, Parque Islas Canarias, Arrecife ☎ 928 80 00 00 🕓 Daily 1–3, 8–11:30

Puerto Bahía (€–€€)
Sit at a table overlooking the old port and watch the sun turn the sea red

as it sets among the volcanoes. This restaurant on a terrace specializes in fresh fish and seafood.

✉ Avenida de Varadero 5, Puerto del Carmen ☎ 928 51 37 93 🕐 All day

Mirador del Río (€)

Manrique's starting point when constructing this spectacular site was the bar-restaurant, and the *mirador* is essentially nothing more than a café with a view. Drinks, light snacks and a fine setting.

✉ About 7km (4 miles) north of Haría ☎ 928 52 65 48 🕐 Daily 10–5:45

Mirador de la Valle (€€)

Enjoy a basic snack at this simple viewpoint location looking clear across the Haría valley. Approach slowly – the *mirador* is half-way round a hairpin bend.

✉ Los Valles, on the road south of Haría ☎ 928 52 80 36 🕐 Lunch; closed Mon

FUERTEVENTURA
Bahía La Pared (€€)

Book a table on the terrace in the early evening at this beachside restaurant to enjoy superb panoramic views of the sunset and coastline. There's also a children's playground and a swimming pool with waterslides.

✉ Playa de la Pared ☎ 928 54 90 30 🕐 Lunch, dinner

Mirador de Morro Veloso (€–€€)

There are mesmerizing views of the island's moonscape from this viewpoint restaurant, which serves good local cuisine.

✉ 2km (1.2 miles) north of Betancuria ☎ 928 17 40 87 🕐 Daily 10–5

César Manrique designs

Local boy César Manrique (1919–92), an international figure in the world of modern art, was fascinated by man's relationship with landscape, and was eager to ensure that mass tourism on his beloved Lanzarote took place with respect for local culture and tradition. He campaigned energetically, and successfully, for the environment and sustainable tourism. No new buildings may be more than two storeys; he banned all roadside billboards; he took over Lanzarote's geographical oddities and with sheer brilliance turned them into extraordinary attractions.

Jameos del Agua (➤ 46–47)
Museo Internacional de Arte Contemporáneo (➤ 37)
Cueva de los Verdes (➤ 38–39)
Mirador del Río (➤ 50–51)
El Diablo restaurant, Timanfaya (➤ 60)
Monumento al Campesino (➤ 122–123)
Jardín de Cactus, Guatiza (➤ 48–49)
Fundación César Manrique, Taro de Tahíche (➤ 42–43)

Manrique mobiles
Manrique's mischievous inventiveness strikes a chord with the youngest art-lovers when they see his mad mobiles, standing at junctions and roundabouts like giant coloured toys whirling in the wind. See if you can spot the one at the airport as soon as you arrive in Lanzarote.

Exploring

Lanzarote, devastated by volcanic explosions and blanketed with lava, has so much to interest and amaze that every outing seems to be interrupted by constant photo stops. Some sights are the product of the power of nature, some are man-made, and some a combination of the two. It's fascinating to see how man's inventiveness has turned the volcanic activity to his advantage, especially the covering of vast areas of good soil with *picón*, black volcanic grit that absorbs any moisture and helps crops flourish.

After the tidy lines of Lanzarote, the dusty streets and barren landscapes of Fuerteventura are quite a contrast. Away from the resorts, the island offers a natural untamed beauty; ancient mountain ranges and jagged black rocks trimmed by deep dry ravines and coastlines softened by soft white sands blown in from the Sahara.

Northern Lanzarote

The north of Lanzarote boasts the island's most spectacular man-made sights, and the man responsible for the majority of them is César Manrique. You can trace much of his life story within the loop that makes up the main roads of the north: from his boyhood holidays in Famara to his last resting place in Haría.

Teguise

The area has some of the best views on the island, courtesy of its many *miradores*. Here you will find stark natural contrasts in a very small area, from the lush oasis that is the Haría valley and the El Jable desert around Famara, to the stark lichen-covered *malpaís* and the cultivated lava fields around Monte Corona. There's also a contrast in cultures from the Robinson-Crusoe island of La Graciosa to the *centros comerciales* (shopping centres) and British pubs of Costa Teguise. The ancient island capital of Teguise is possibly the most beautiful small town in the Canaries; quiet, dignified and lovingly restored.

ARRIETA

Arrieta is a relatively undeveloped, traditional small town of simple, low, white houses on the island's northeast coast; it is little known to visitors but nevertheless makes a good lunch stop after a trip to the nearby Jameos del Agua (➤ 46–47) or Cueva de los Verdes (➤ 38–39). Its attractions include one of several fine beaches to be found along this part of the coast, and a picturesque harbour with a quay made of volcanic rock.

➕ 11F ✉ 22km (13.5 miles) north of Arrecife 🍴 El Charcón (€; ➤ 101), Arrieta waterfront 🚌 Four times a day from Arrecife

CASTILLO DE SANTA BÁRBARA (OR GUANAPAY) AND MUSEO DEL EMIGRANTE CANARIO

A fine castle standing proudly on the summit of volcanic Mount Guanapay, overlooking the little town of Teguise, the Castillo de Santa Bárbara was for centuries a vital defence against Moorish raiders, who came inland as far as the island's old capital. The fortress was first erected in the 14th century by Lancelotto Malocello, the voyager who gave his name to the island, reconstructed 100 years later by Maciot de Béthencourt, and further strengthened in the 16th century.

Distinctive for its pale golden stone on an island where almost everything is either black or white, the castle dominates the area of villa developments around Oasis de Nazaret. The views alone amply reward a visit.

Inside the castle today an emigrant museum tells the stirring, sometimes tragic, story of how the poorest Canary Islanders have left in search of a better life. During certain periods in the past, the people of Lanzarote emigrated en masse to South America. Among other things, we learn that natives of different Canary Islands settled in different countries. Lanzaroteños went mainly to Venezuela, while people from Fuerteventura emigrated to Cuba.

www.teguise.com

🚶 7B ✉ 1.3km (1 mile) up a steep gravel track northwest of Teguise ☎ 686 47 03 70 🕐 May–Oct daily 10–4; Nov–Apr Tue–Fri 10–5, Sat, Mon 10–4
✋ Inexpensive 🍴 La Bodeguita de Teguise (€€), Calle Dácil, Teguise
🚌 No 7 takes around 20 mins from Arrecife to Teguise, 6 buses a day Mon–Fri, 3–4 a day Sat–Sun

COSTA TEGUISE

Within a few years this carefully planned, purpose-built resort town has sprung up alongside excellent beaches 5km (3 miles) up the coast from Arrecife. The quality of the accommodation and facilities is above average for the Canaries, and represents good value for money, so the area now attracts a lot of holidaymakers, many of them families looking for self-catering options.

Costa Teguise has also proved attractive to Spanish celebrities, a number of whom have holiday homes here. But the resort feels unfocused and has an unfinished look in parts. It is a narrow ribbon development with three different focal points (Bastian, Jabillo and Cucharas). Obviously there is no 'old quarter', and a string of *centros comerciales* (shopping centres) and holiday apartment blocks backs onto the beach. Although everything is low-rise and has broadly been guided by the principles laid down by César Manrique, the new buildings can appear charmless.

Yet what the resort lacks in history or character is made up for by a location ideal for sun, sea, sand, sport and sightseeing.

As well as the main Las Cucharas beach there are other waterfront areas, including a sandy beach at Jabillo. Watersports facilities and rentals are available, and there is also an aquapark (➤ 72). An 18-hole golf course (➤ 108) is to the north of town.

✚ 8C ✉ On the coast 7km (4 miles) northwest of Arrecife 🍴 Restaurants, cafés and bars (€–€€€) at all three main beach areas 🚌 No 1 from Arrecife every 20 mins throughout the day Mon–Fri, every 30 mins at weekends and festivals. Journey takes 20 mins

CUEVA DE LOS VERDES
Best places to see,
➤ 38–39.

FAMARA

Most tourist development has been on the sheltered southern and eastern coasts of the island, but the north coast has some glorious golden sandy beaches too. One of the very best on the north coast is Playa de Famara – so good that visitors are prepared to put up with the slightly more temperamental weather and that little bit of extra wind that comes from the northwest. The ocean currents are also more dangerous here, so swimming and diving are discouraged, although windsurfers are drawn to this beach.

At one end of the beach, La Caleta de Famara – a small, working fishing village and low-key resort – makes for an enjoyable stroll, or even a good place to stay on this side of the island. It is particularly popular with anglers.

Rising behind the shore towards the other end of the beach, the Riscos de Famara (Famara Cliffs) reach a height of almost 450m (1,475ft). These cliffs, with their exquisite sea views out towards Graciosa Island (➤ 94–95), continue – under different names – as far as the Mirador del Río (➤ 50–51) and beyond.

✚ 7A ✉ 11km (7 miles) north of Teguise 🍴 Several simple restaurants (€)
🚌 No 18 runs 4 times a day between La Caleta and Arrecife

FUNDACIÓN CÉSAR MANRIQUE

Best places to see, ➤ 42–43.

GUINATE PARQUE TROPICAL (GUINATE TROPICAL PARK)

The Tropical Park near Guinate is enjoyable and entertaining with more than 1,300 species of exotic birds and animals. Ten rare Humboldt penguins are the latest addition. Meerkats, monkeys, otters and macaws live in a landscape of waterfalls and lakes.

✚ 10E ✉ Guinate (4km/2.5 miles from Haría) ☎ 928 83 55 00
🕐 Daily 10–5 ✋ Expensive 🚌 Join an excursion organized from your resort, or go by car

HARÍA

In contrast to Lanzarote's clichéd image as a volcanic island with a lunar landscape, here in the north of the island is a delightful little hill town in a lush green valley. Surprisingly, it is perfectly tranquil and unspoiled, with few visitors. The narrow streets and lanes are speckled with colour where purple bougainvillaea and red pelargoniums cover brilliant white walls. Stroll past some fine houses and pretty corners to reach a main square shaded by a canopy of leafy branches and loud with sparrows.

The setting of the village is especially striking, among a cool, green patchwork of fields and wildflower meadows shaded by palm trees. Poetically, this has been dubbed the Valley of 1,000 Palms – or even, sometimes, the Valley of 10,000 Palms! Some dispute the locals' claim that they have more palm trees here than anywhere else in the Canaries, but many plant species do grow in this valley that botanists have not found on any other Canary Island. You will also see several types of cactus.

One of the best places to get an overview of this haven is from the Mirador de Haría, a high viewpoint beside the twisting main road as it hairpins round the heights of the Galería de Famara some 5km (3 miles) south of Haría.

➕ 10F ✉ 15km (9 miles) north of Teguise 🍴 Snack bars (€) on the southern edge of town 🚌 No 7 from Arrecife ❓ Fiesta de San Juan celebrates midsummer on 24 Jun. It is preceeded by 2 or 3 days of events

a walk around La Graciosa

Take the 10am ferry from Lanzarote to La Graciosa, which takes 20 minutes to reach the tiny port of Caleta del Sebo. The walk takes in Las Agujas (The Needles) and the Pedro Barba ridge, which form a mountain at the centre of the island, as well as panoramic views and stetches of deserted beaches.

Walk along the quayside, then turn right (at the bar) on a footpath and take the dirt road towards the Pedro Barba ridge.

La Graciosa's two volcanoes stand either side of the track: Mojón to the left and Pedro Barba to the right. The third

peak between them is Montaña Clara, a separate island. Behind is a fine view of the village of Caleta del Sebo and the cliffs of Famara.

At a fork keep right and head towards the holiday homes at Pedro Barba.

You are walking around the foot of Pedro Barba volcano. The rocky island of Alegranza comes into view.

Where the track forks again continue on the left (the right-hand path heads down to Pedro Barba village).

The track skirts the northern slopes of Pedro Barba, with dunes away to the right, and a sea view of Alegranza. Ahead rises Montaña Bermeja, and the cone of Pedro Barba comes into view again.

As the track heads away from Pedro Barba and towards the foot of Montaña Bermeja, take a turn on the left which leads you back in the direction of Lanzarote.

On the right is a spectacular beach of black rock and golden sand, called Playa de las Conchas. Ahead is the dramatic coast of Lanzarote.

A left turn takes the track south, again between Mojón and Pedro Barba. Follow the track back to Caleta del Sebo.

Distance 18km (11 miles) **Time** 4 hours
Start point Caleta del Sebo ✚ 10D 🚢 From Orzola at 10am
🚌 To Orzola leaves Arrecife at 7:40am
End point Caleta del Sebo ✚ 10D 🚢 Back to Orzola at 4pm
🚌 To Arrecife leaves Orzola at 4:30pm
Lunch Simple fish restaurants (€–€€) ✉ Caleta del Sebo

ISLA GRACIOSA

La Graciosa is the tranquil island that rests at the centre of the view from the Mirador del Río (➤ 50–51). For many who come to admire it, this is as near as they get to the island. However, La Graciosa is easily reached and a trip makes an enjoyable day out from Lanzarote.

The channel (El Río) between the two islands is just 2km (1 mile) wide, though the ferry goes the long way round and takes 20 minutes. With a total area of only 41sq km (16sq miles), the island is small enough for keen walkers to circumnavigate in a day. Strong Atlantic currents make it dangerous to swim here.

The island has two sleepy fishing villages. Caleta del Sebo (literally 'Greasy Cove', named after the whale blubber found on the beach) and Pedro Barba are both on the channel between the two islands. There are also superb golden sandy beaches and a couple of simple bar-restaurants and basic *pensiones*. The view from La Graciosa towards the Riscos de Famara and Mirador del Río is almost as good as the view from Lanzarote. Four-by-four taxis can be hired, as well as bikes, from Caleta del Sebo

Away from the shore, La Graciosa consists of dunes and treeless volcanic terrain. Despite this, it was at La Graciosa that

Norman conqueror Jean de Béthencourt first stepped ashore after his journey from Europe.

🕂 10C ✉ 2km (1mile) off northern shore of Lanzarote 🍴 Two basic bar-restaurants (€) at Caleta del Sebo, near the ferry terminal 🚌 No 9 leaves Arrecife at 7:40am to reach Orzola in time for the 10am ferry to La Graciosa. Return to Arrecife on the 4:30pm bus from Orzola ⛴ The daily morning ferry departs Orzola at 10am, noon, 5pm, and 6:30pm (summer only) and returns from La Caleta del Sebo at 8am, 11am, 4pm, and 6pm (summer only) (➤ 28). Don't miss the last boat – unless you want to spend the night on the island

around northern Lanzarote

a drive

This trip takes you through a part of Lanzarote that is both dramatic and pretty. It involves driving down a steep mountain pass. Don't do this drive on Sunday, as the Teguise market brings thousands of people onto this route.

From Arrecife take the main road to Teguise. Note the Manrique sculptures at the junction before Tahíche. César Manrique's extraordinary home is nearby (➤ 42–43).

Except for a strip of *malpaís* to the left of the road, most visible at Tahíche, the countryside is rolling hills of grass and, in spring, abundant wild flowers. As you approach Teguise, the hill of Guanapay, topped by Santa Bárbara Castle (➤ 84–85) comes into view. Teguise (➤ 52–53) deserves a leisurely visit on foot.

Follow the road to Haría, which soon begins to really climb and wind before descending to the town.

On the high plateaux and peaks there are windmills – not the picturesque, old-fashioned kind, but modern wind generators. The high, winding road is airy and enjoyable to drive along, with many outstanding views. In particular, beside a bar-restaurant at a mountain pass, is the beautiful viewpoint called Mirador de Haría (➤ 90). The descent into the green valley of Haría, dotted with palms, is delightful.

Now straighter, the road continues to Ye. Turn left here to Mirador del Río.

The Mirador del Río (➤ 50–51) deserves a stop. A narrow road to the left of the viewpoint is now closed to vehicles and makes a thrilling clifftop stroll.

Turn south again, at first on the same road; then after 2km (1 mile) take a left fork and wind sharply downhill towards the coast.

Jameos del Agua (➤ 46–47) and Cueva de los Verdes (➤ 38–39) are nearby and well worth a visit.

Turn right onto the coast road, which skirts Arrieta (➤ 84), crosses the cactus fields and passes in front of the entrance of the Jardín de Cactus (➤ 48–49). At Tahíche, turn left to return to Arrecife.

Distance 66km (41 miles)
Time 5 hours
Start/end point Arrecife ✚ 7D
Lunch El Charcón (€; ➤ 101), Arrieta waterfront

JAMEOS DEL AGUA
Best places to see, ➤ 46–47.

JARDÍN DE CACTUS
Best places to see, ➤ 48–49.

MIRADOR DEL RÍO
Best places to see, ➤ 50–51.

ORZOLA
Close to the northern tip of Lanzarote, on the edge of the *malpaís* formed by La Corona volcano, this little working fishing harbour is

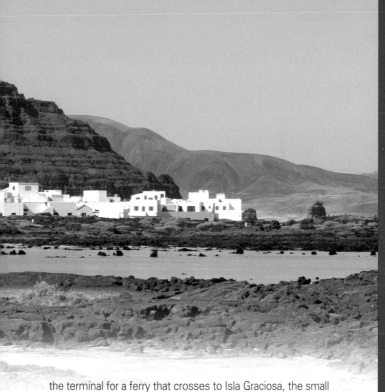

the terminal for a ferry that crosses to Isla Graciosa, the small island facing the Mirador del Río (➤ 50–51). Orzola makes a good base for keen anglers, while it's also an excellent lunch stop if you avoid the more obvious tourist restaurants. There are good beaches nearby, too.

✚ 11D ✉ 37km (23 miles) north of Arrecife 🍴 Restaurante Punta Fariones (€€), just off the harbour 🚌 No 9 from Arrecife at 7:40am daily. Leaves Orzola for Arrecife at 4:30pm 🚢 Ferries at 10am, noon, 5pm and 6:30pm, summer only, to Isla Graciosa (➤ 94–95)

TEGUISE
Best places to see, ➤ 52–53.

HOTELS

COSTA TEGUISE
Beatriz Costa & Spa (€€€)
This huge hotel is some distance from the sea and the resort's centre. Black, white and red marble in the cool, spacious public areas reflects Lanzarote's colours. Amazing atria have waterfalls, a stream and lush tropical greenery. Outside, a large swimming area has several pools. It also has a spa and thalassotherapy centre.
✉ Calle Atalaya ☎ 928 59 08 28; www.beatrizhoteles.com

Casa Carlos (€€)
Lovely, modern, three-bedroom villa with private heated swimming pool and maid service. It's in a quiet area, yet close to the beach and the centre of the resort. Very reasonably priced.
✉ Calle Isla de Lobos ☎ 01463 731 245 (UK); www.casacarlos.co.uk

Gran Meliá Salinas (€€€)
This stylish, luxurious hotel overlooks Las Cucharas beach. With a superb cactus garden in front, the hotel encircles wonderful watery tropical gardens inside. Rooms and villas are of the highest standard, with beautiful bathrooms and sea views, and there are several restaurants.
✉ Avenida Islas Canarias ☎ 928 59 00 40; www.solmelia.com

Los Zocos Club Resort (€)
Choose between hotel or self-catering accommodation at this popular family holiday complex near the beach. There's an attractive pool area, restaurants, sports facilities, landscaped grounds and plenty of amusements for all age groups, including a children's club and programmes for sports and other activities.
✉ Avenida Islas Canarias 15 ☎ 928 59 21 22, www.loszocos.com

HARÍA
Villa Lola y Juan (€€)
For an away-from-it-all experience, stay at this rural aparthotel, set on a farm and surrounded by fruit orchards and vineyards. Choose

from a four-bedroom house and two apartments – one with kitchen and all with their own terrace. Outside is an extensive sun terrace and a heated swimming pool.

✉ Calle Fajardo 16 ☎ 928 83 52 56, www.villalolayjuan.com

RESTAURANTS

ARRIETA
El Charcón (€)
This simple, waterside restaurant specializes in fresh fish and seafood. The mussels come with an exquisite marinara sauce, the grilled squid melts in your mouth and the bargain set menu includes three courses and a glass of wine.

✉ Arrieta Wharf ☎ 928 84 81 10 🕐 Lunch, dinner; closed Mon

Jameos del Agua (€€)
When César Manrique turned this bizarre volcanic feature into a major tourist attraction, he added snack bars and a restaurant serving excellent Canarian cuisine.

✉ Jameos del Agua, 2km (1 mile) from Arrieta ☎ 928 84 80 24 🕐 Snack bars open 10–6:30; restaurant Tue, Fri–Sat 7:30pm–11:30pm

El Lago (€€)
About 10 minutes' walk from the town centre along the shore road, the restaurant has a fine sea view and offers a range of shellfish, fish and meat dishes.

✉ On seafront north of harbour ☎ 928 84 81 76 🕐 Mon–Sat noon–9.30pm, Sun noon–5pm

LA CALETA DE FAMARA
Las Bajas (€)
Basic, but popular, meat and fish dishes, both international and local, are served at this simple but charming eating place on the edge of a genuine, north-coast fishing village.

✉ Avenida Marinero 25 ☎ 928 52 86 17 🕐 Daily 9–9

Casa Ramón (€)

Many visitors pause for a simple Spanish lunch of fried fish, paella or pasta at this bar-restaurant beside the road into the village.

✉ Calle Callejón ☎ 928 52 85 23 🕐 Lunch, dinner; closed Tue and Jun

COSTA TEGUISE

Costa Teguise has three distinct dining areas: Playa de las Cucharas, in the north of the resort; the busier area around Playa del Jabillo (including Plaza Pueblo Martinero); and the smaller Playa Bastián area at the southern end of town. There is a short drive between each district, and taxis ply between them constantly.

Bar Bastián Restaurant (€€)

Sit on the terrace, order a meal or a drink, and enjoy the sea views from this tourist-orientated beachside brasserie. Open all day (it serves breakfast as well as lunch and dinner), there's often entertainment such as live music, quizzes and satellite TV for sports fans.

✉ Avenida del Mar ☎ 928 59 05 79 🕐 Daily 9:30am–midnight

Casa Blanca (€€)

In a charming little detached building with a hexagonal roof, this unusual grill restaurant in the Jablillo area has an open kitchen and dark wooden tables on an enclosed terrace. Local fish dishes, salads and steak with peppercorns are among the choices.

✉ 4 Calle Las Olas ☎ 928 59 01 55 🕐 Dinner

La Chimenea (€€)

Good Italian food at the main beach. Relaxing decor of cool green and white motif outside, warmer orange and white inside.

✉ Centro Comercial Las Cucharas ☎ 928 59 08 37 🕐 Daily 8.30am–11.30pm; closed Thu

Domus Pompei (€€)

This popular, family-run place has a very Italian menu of classic dishes well prepared and served in pleasant surroundings.

✉ Calle Tabaiba 2 ☎ 928 82 71 12 🕐 Lunch, dinner

La Graciosa (€€€)

Gran Meliá Salinas, the smartest hotel on the island (➤ 100), has an elegant restaurant open to the public. Entering on a walkway through tropical gardens and over ponds where goldfish swim adds to the ambience. The food is sophisticated and mainly French, with giant prawns, or sole with scallop mousse. Wonderful desserts. Live music.

✉ Avenida Islas Canarias ☎ 928 59 00 40 🕓 Dinner; closed Sun, Mon

Mesón La Jordana (€€€)

See page 61.

Mesón de la Villa (€€)

An open wood fire is used to cook some of the excellent fish and meat dishes served at this friendly and enjoyable restaurant, ideally placed on the waterfront.

✉ Plaza del Pueblo Marinero ☎ 928 34 62 71 🕓 All day

Montmartre Bistro (€€€)

A neon 'Moulin Rouge' on the roof is a reminder of the real Montmartre, as are the quarry-tiled floor, oil lamps and pink and white table-cloths. Fine French cooking, such as duck liver pâté and chicken stuffed with prawns served with white wine sauce.

✉ Avenida de las Palmeras, near Calle Los Geranios ☎ 928 59 12 05
🕓 Dinner; closed Thu

Neptuno (€€)

Tucked away in the little plaza at the seafront end of Avenue de Jabillo, this relaxed but stylish bar-restaurant is favoured by well-to-do locals rather than tourists. Concentrating on well-prepared fish and seafood dishes, the cooking has a French/Italian slant, and good local wines are served.

✉ Centro Comercial Neptuno, Avenida de Jabillo ☎ 928 59 03 78 🕓 Lunch, dinner; closed Sun

El Pescador (€€)

Alongside a busy pedestrian plaza, this friendly restaurant invites you to come inside and shut out the noise. Good service and an emphasis on seafood.

✉ Plaza Pueblo Marinero ☎ 928 59 08 74 ⏰ Lunch, dinner

El Portón (€€)

The friendly staff at this authentic Spanish bar will help you choose from a selection of good-value *tapas* (with prices starting at €1.50) or full meals.

✉ Calle Las Olas ☎ 928 59 08 71 ⏰ Lunch, dinner; closed Sun

Villa Toledo (€€)

Enjoy cocktails on the terrace of the oldest house in Costa Teguise, with wonderful sea views. The full menu has an emphasis on fish and Canarian specialities with an Italian twist, with something to suit everyone.

✉ Avenida Los Cocederos s/n ☎ 928 59 06 26 ⏰ Lunch, dinner

HARÍA
Casal Cura (€€)

See page 60.

El Cortijo de Haría (€€)

In an attractive, whitewashed, converted farmhouse set back from the road, this lively and popular grill restaurant serves classic dishes from Lanzarote.

✉ Calle El Palmeral 5, on the Teguise road, at the edge of Haría
☎ 928 83 52 65 ⏰ 11–8 (lunch only if reserved)

Mirador del Río (€)

See page 77.

Mirador de la Valle (€€)

See page 77.

ISLA GRACIOSA
El Marinero (€)
Visitors to the island can find food and refreshment at this bar-restaurant near the ferry terminal. Fresh fish and local wines are the specialities.

✉ Calle García Escámez 14, Caleta del Sebo ☎ 928 84 20 70 🕐 Lunch, dinner

NAZARET
Lagomar (€€)
This restaurant is in an extraordinary setting, carved into cliffs and connected to the ground by a tunnel and steps, with gardens, caves, a lake and walkways. Choose from imaginative meat, fish and vegetarian dishes, mainly French and Italian in inspiration.

✉ Calle Loros 6, on the main road between Tahíche and Teguise ☎ 928 84 56 65; www.lag-o-mar.com 🕐 Tue–Sat noon–midnight, Sun noon–6pm

ORZOLA
Bahía de Orzola (€€)
Blue and white cloths and paintwork mirror the marine location of this popular fish restaurant right on the dockside.

✉ Calle La Quemadita 1 ☎ 928 84 25 75 🕐 Lunch, dinner

Casa Arraez (€)
Rough red-painted tables made from old rope spools stand on the quayside at this restaurant, which looks like a tatty fisherman's shack. Sample the good-value set meal of Canarian stew and dessert, with bread and wine.

✉ Calle La Quemadita 15 ☎ 928 84 25 86 🕐 Lunch; closed Thu

Punta Fariones (€–€€)
See page 61.

TEGUISE
Acatife (€€)
Ambitious and delicious cooking such as cucumber soup with smoked salmon, rabbit in red wine, charcoal-grilled meat, and local wines, served in a restored historic building.

✉ Calle San Miguel 4 ☎ 928 84 50 37 🕒 Lunch, dinner; closed Sun–Mon

Bodega Santa Bárbara (€)
Tucked away behind the church, this pleasant café-cum-*tapas*-bar shares a modern but traditional-style building with a few shops and an art gallery, and has an attractive courtyard terrace on two levels.

✉ Calle Cruz 5 ☎ 928 84 52 00 🕒 Lunch; closed Sat

Ikarus (€€€)
French-style cooking of fish and meat dishes, plus a good wine list and a romantic bistro atmosphere.

✉ Plaza del 18 de Julio ☎ 928 84 53 32 🕒 Lunch, dinner; closed Sun dinner and Mon

YE
El Volcán (€€)
This big, cheerful, country-style restaurant is situated in the hills near Mirador del Río. Try the great mixed starter of *gofio*, figs, dried fish, sweet potatoes and goat's cheese.

✉ Plaza de los Remedios 4 ☎ 928 83 01 56 🕒 10–5; closed Sat

SHOPPING

MARKETS
Teguise
The main shopping event for many visitors is the large Sunday market in Teguise. Thousands of tourists arrive by bus from resorts all around the island and others come by car or on foot. On sale are goods made mostly for tourists, including souvenirs and a fair amount of fakes. Teguise is no longer an authentic market, but is worth a visit if you don't mind crowds. The atmosphere is enhanced by colourful folklore shows and traditional events.

✉ Teguise 🕒 Sun 9am–2pm

Costa Teguise

This is a much smaller version of Teguise's Sunday market.

✉ Plaza Pueblo Marinero 🕐 Fri from 6pm onwards

ENTERTAINMENT

ARRIETA
Jameos del Agua

After dark on Tuesday, Friday and Saturday, these water caverns in the north of the island become a popular nightclub, where crowds drink, dine and dance in the extraordinary underground setting (➤ 46–47).

✉ Near Arrieta, 26km (16 miles) north of Arrecife ☎ 928 84 80 20 🕐 Tue, Fri–Sat 7pm–1:45am

COSTA TEGUISE

Costa Teguise is really the only resort in the north that offers a full choice of discos and bars that stay open late. The Baobab Club (2nd floor, Centro Comercial Teguise Playa, Jabillo) is one popular haunt here. Many hotels offer entertainment most evenings from about 10pm until midnight. There's no need to be a guest at the hotel. Check the weekly programme displayed at hotels and make your choice. Try the Gran Meliá Salinas hotel (➤ 100).

SPORT

CYCLING
Bike Station

Good-quality bikes with child seats, plus delivery to your hotel.

✉ CC Maretas (near post office), Costa Teguise ☎ 628 10 21 77; www.mylanzarote.com

Tommy's Bikes

The leading and longest established rental shop for top-quality touring, racing and mountain bikes. This friendly, helpful company gives free advice and maps, and recommends and organizes island tours and excursions. A typical excursion lasts a whole day, including jeep transfers, bikes, water, tour guide and boat transfers where necessary.

☒ Calle de la Galeta 16, Galeón Playa (near Playa del Jabillo), Costa Teguise
☎ 928 59 20 13; www.tommys-bikes.com ⏰ Closed Sun

DIVING
Calipso Diving
Top-quality diving for all levels (minimum age 12).
☒ Centro Comercial Nautical, Local 3, Avenida Islas Canarias, Costa Teguise
☎ 928 59 08 79; www.calipso-diving.com

Diving Lanzarote
High-quality scuba diving centre on Las Cucharas Beach, with a
variety of rental and excursion options, including night diving.
☒ Playa de las Cucharas, Costa Teguise ☎ 928 59 04 07

GOLF
Club de Golf de Costa Teguise
The tender green turf of the 18-hole, par-72 course looks dazzling
amid the dark hills, cacti and palms within sight of the Atlantic. No
handicap is required. The course offers a driving range, putting and
pitching greens, buggy, trolley and club rental, and a club house.
Lessons are available.
☒ 2km (1 mile) up Avenida del Golf, Costa Teguise ☎ 928 59 05 12;
www.lanzarote-golf.com

WALKING
Canary Trekking
Guided walks and mountain-biking trips on La Graciosa and other
parts of the island, with a nature guide.
☒ Calle La Laguna 8, Casa 1, Costa Teguise ☎ 609 53 76 84

WINDSURFING
Windsurfing Club Nathalie Simon
Courses and equipment rental at this windsurfing centre at Playa
de las Cucharas. Canoes also for rent.
☒ CC Puerto Tahíche, Local 18, Calle Las Olas, Costa Teguise ☎ 928 59
07 31; www.sportaway-lanzarote.com

Central and Southern Lanzarote

Central Lanzarote is dominated by the island's capital Arrecife, and the tourist hotspot of Puerto del Carmen, while in the south, the island's contrasting landscapes are at their most impressive: from the infernal landscape of Timanfaya's *malpaís* to the golden Playa de Papagayo.

Arrecife

For a feel of contemporary Lanzarote, spend a day in Arrecife or hop on a waterbus to Puerto Calero, where the marina attracts a well-heeled clientele. If you head out of town to the rural heart, the central part of the island can offer culture and history as well. A growing number of people are choosing to make their holiday base here, in the *casas rurales* and *hoteles rurales* (country houses and rural hotels). There is nowhere else on Lanzarote that is remotely as beautiful as the Papagayo sands, although the Fire Mountains of the Parque Nacional de Timanfaya are the main attraction in the south. A visit to the vineyards of La Geria is the island's most unexpected visual

treat; a remarkable example of man's ingenuity in the face of adversity. The saltpans of Janubio are another example of how the islanders have successfully harnessed the elements, creating a semi-natural work of art.

ARRECIFE

Until the last century Arrecife was no more than a small working
port. Inland Teguise was the island's capital and market centre,
well away from the raiders who harried the coast. That's why
Arrecife is still known to many locals simply as *el puerto* (the port).
To protect itself, Arrecife built the two fine fortresses that still
watch over its harbours today. As the coastal danger declined and
trade increased, Arrecife grew, finally becoming the capital of
Lanzarote in 1852.

If, while touring Lanzarote, you ever wonder 'Where is
everybody?', the answer is, 'in Arrecife'. Today around half the
islanders live in the capital, and many more come here to work
each day. A striking, in some ways rather satisfying, contrast to
the picturesque strangeness of the rest of the island, Arrecife is an
ordinary, hardworking Spanish town making few concessions to
tourists. Having expanded well before the days of César Manrique,
this is the one place on the island that really does not conform to
his aesthetic guidelines. Indeed, Lanzarote's most unsightly
modern buildings are here.

There are pretty spots, such as the town's excellent El Reducto main beach and its old harbour, with the waterside gardens and promenade. The other places of interest, too, are all close to the sea, and the main tourist office is also here on Blas Cabrera Felipe (➤ 30). A coastal path heading south means that you can walk all the way to Puerto del Carmen – past the airport.

✠ 7D

Castillo de San Gabriel

Poised on a tiny islet called Islote de los Ingleses, just off the main town-centre old harbour, Castillo de San Gabriel adds charm to Arrecife's waterfront. It was built in 1590 by Italian architect Leonardo Torriani on part of the string of rocky islets off the town, and became a vital part of the defences protecting the harbour and town from marauding pirates. A low, sturdy, square and rather

featureless structure, the castle is made more appealing by its honey-coloured stonework and the islet setting.

One of the most endearing features of the castle today – though it once had a serious military function – is that to reach it you must walk out along a walled breakwater, which serves as a pedestrian causeway. A second causeway gives access for permitted vehicles. It passes over a small drawbridge, known as the Puente de las Bolas – the Bridge of the Balls – because of the two cannon balls perched on top.

Some weatherbeaten old cannons stand outside the castle. The view back towards the harbour and promenade puts Arrecife in a better light, with the white-capped San Ginés church belfry and the whitewashed houses of the little town standing out against the volcanic terrain beyond.

A small archaeological museum inside the castle has an assortment of historic items discovered locally, such as fossils and Guanche art.

✚ *Arrecife 4d* ✉ Avenida Gen Franco ☎ 928 80 28 84 🕐 Currently closed for renovation ✋ Inexpensive 🍽 Cafés (€) in Calle Leon y Castillo 🚌 From Avenida Gen Franco

El Charco de San Ginés

Sometimes mistakenly thought by visitors to be the name of Arrecife's old harbour, the Charco lies back from the sea within the town centre. This curious little lake or lagoon of sea water, surrounded by a walkway and modest fishermen's cottages, is said to lie at the very origin of Arrecife. The legendary San Ginés lived here as a hermit beside the water. A village of pious fishing folk grew around the hermitage and, as the village expanded into a town, the hermitage became the town's church. There are several such lagoons around the Lanzarote coastline, for example Salinas de Janubio (► 144) and El Charco north of Costa Teguise (► 86–87); these have been put to use as salt pans, producing a coarse salt for preserving fish.

✝ *Arrecife 4a* ✉ Avenida Vargas ✋ Free 🍴 Cafés (€) on waterfront
🚌 From Avenida La Marina

Iglesia de San Ginés

Arrecife's main church, this dignified little building of dark volcanic
stone and bright white paintwork is dedicated to the town's patron
saint. It was built in the 18th century when Arrecife was no more
than a harbour village. Handsomely restored, the church is still at
the old heart of the town, standing at one end of a pleasant
square. Restoration has given the church a facelift and inside, it
has an attractive Moorish ceiling. Formerly the hermitage of Ginés,
it stands beside the El Charco lagoon. The locals' devotion to San
Ginés is part of the town's marine tradition.

✝ *Arrecife 4b* ✉ Plaza de San Ginés 🕓 Open to public daily 9–1, 5–7,
except during church services ✋ Free 🚌 From Avenida La Marina
❓ Fiesta de San Ginés in August with parades and traditional dancing
in the streets

a walk around Arrecife

The relaxed little capital of Lanzarote is where the real, modern life of the island is lived. Start at the tourist information office on the waterfront, an attractive pavilion made of volcanic stone and carved timbers.

Walk north, with the sea on your right, along the promenade as far as Calle de León y Castillo. Turn right into the short street Calle Ginés de Castro y Alverez.

This leads to the plaza and church dedicated to San Ginés, Arrecife's patron saint (▶ 112–113).

Follow the white-washed lanes to El Charco de San Ginés (► 112–113). Follow the quiet promenade that runs all the way round the Charco, including a bridge across the entrance to the lagoon.

At the inland end of the lagoon, short lanes lead back to Calle León y Castillo.

Turn left into Calle de León y Castillo, towards the sea. Turn right at Calle Gen Goded and follow the traffic along Calle Alferez Cabrera Tavio to Plaza de la Constitución. Cross the square to the far corner and turn left and right into Calle Luis Morote and follow this back street, with its glimpses of the sea.

On a busy corner dozens of café tables are set out beside Calle Dr Negrín. Ahead you can see the five-star Gran Hotel, Lanzarote's tallest (and ugliest) building that is well worth a stop for a cocktail in its 17th-floor bar.

Turn left along Avenida Mancomunidad. The road turns right and left to approach the promenade gardens and the tourist information pavilion.

Distance 5km (3 miles)
Time 2 hours
Start/end point Tourist office ✚ *Arrecife 3d* ✉ Avenida la Marina
Lunch Bars and restaurants (€–€€) along Calle de León y Castillo

More to see in Central and Southern Lanzarote

ÁGUILA

Standing on a promontory called Punta del Águila (Eagle Point), between the beautiful Playa Blanca and Playa de Papagayo beaches on the island's southern shore, the restored circular watchtower called Castillo de las Coloradas (or Torre del Águila – Eagle Tower) stands guard beside the beach where de Béthencourt is said to have made his first landing on Lanzarote in 1402 (even though he had already arrived at El Río and visited the

island of La Graciosa). Another local story is that de Béthencourt himself erected the tower, but it was built much later; it bears the date of 1769. The present structure dates from 1778. There are good views from here across the straits to Fuerteventura.

✚ 2F ✉ 1km (0.5 miles) from Playa Blanca ☻ Free access ∜ Bars and restaurants (€–€€) on waterfront in Playa Blanca

CASTILLO DE SAN JOSÉ
Best places to see, ➤ 36–37.

ERMITA DE LOS DOLORES (HERMITAGE OF THE SORROWS)

Pilgrims flock to this beautiful church in the village of Mancha Blanca, especially on 15 September, the feast day of the Virgin of the Volcanoes. The village stands above the desolate *malpaís* at the point where it meets highly productive, neatly farmed fields layered with *picón*.

The Hermitage of the Sorrows – a gracious building with a cupola and a plain white interior – was built in honour of the Virgin of the Volcanoes, patron saint of Lanzarote, after she apparently saved the village from destruction. It happened during the island's most recent volcanic eruption, in 1824, when lava and fire poured down from the Tinguatón volcano. The blazing liquid crept its way towards the village, igniting all in its path. Local people prayed fervently, begging Our Lady to spare them. The pious say that she listened to their pleas, for the lava flow did come to a halt – stopped, supposedly, by the Virgin's veil – at the very foot of Mancha Blanca village. The exact spot where the Virgin must have stood has been marked by a cross at the edge of the *malpaís*.

Mancha Blanca also has an important National Park Interpretation Centre with a permanent exhibition on the vulcanology of the Canary Islands, and Lanzarote in particular (➤ 134).

✚ 5B ✉ Mancha Blanca 🕓 Open all day every day; locked at night ✋ Donations welcome 🍴 Bar–restaurant (€€) across the road

FEMÉS

This likeable, secluded little village on the back road to Playa Blanca is known locally for its goats, whose milk is used to produce delicious cheese. Perched on a rocky ledge surrounded by hills, there are good views across the Rubicón plain to the south from El Balcón (The Balcony), opposite the church. Serious walkers can enjoy an even better panorama by climbing the Atalaya de Femés, a 609m (1,998ft) volcanic peak with breathtaking views to Timanfaya in one direction and Fuerteventura in the other. Femés was one of the first European settlements on the island, and the village church of San Marcial de Rubicón was the first cathedral to be built in the Canary Islands.

✚ 3E ✉ 5km (3 miles) south of Uga; 8km (5 miles) north of Playa Blanca 🍴 Several restaurants (€–€€) in Playa Blanca 🚌 No 5 between Femés and Arrecife 2–3 times a day Mon–Fri

EL GOLFO

On the southwestern shore of the island, El Golfo (The Golf) is the extraordinary result of a meeting between the blackened volcanic devastation of Timanfaya and the power of the Atlantic waves. Here the half-submerged cone of a volcano has been eroded and transformed into a bizarre natural attraction. Over time, the ocean has eaten into the volcanic crater, leaving a lagoon surrounded by an amphitheatre of lava cliff, the rock streaked and stained with a multitude of strange reds and russets.

Most remarkable is the colour of the lagoon. A number of factors, including volcanic minerals and algae, have given the water a deep, intense emerald hue, especially brilliant when it catches the sun, and a striking contrast to the glorious blue sea that lies beside it. Although linked to the ocean, the lagoon appears quite separate from it – the connection is through volcanic passages hidden underground. In the black volcanic sand you can see small pieces of the green, quartz-like stone called olivina.

To reach the lagoon, follow the access road on the left 2km (1 mile) before the village of El Golfo. On reaching the car park continue on foot, following signs for a short walk around the headland.

Between El Golfo village and the lagoon there are a number of sheltered bays with black beaches. The seashore village of El Golfo itself has rather an end-of-the-road feel, but has become a centre for enticing fish restaurants.

⊞ 2C ✉ 12km (7.5 miles) northwest of Yaiza 👋 Free 🍴 Seafront restaurants (€€) in El Golfo village serve fresh fish and shellfish

ISLOTE DE HILARIO

Best places to see, ➤ 44–45.

LOS HERVIDEROS

On the western shore, where the dark volcanic *malpaís* descends into the blue Atlantic waves, a *mirador* (viewpoint) looks across at a place where the ocean thunders in and out of sea caverns. The turbulent, bubbling effect has been called Los Hervideros, the boiling waters.

✚ 2D ✉ 3km (2 miles) off Yaiza–Playa Blanca road 🍴 Nearby restaurants (€) in El Golfo, Janubio or Yaiza

MONUMENTO AL CAMPESINO AND CASA-MUSEO DEL CAMPESINO (MONUMENT AND MUSEUM HOUSE OF THE FARMER)

The *campesino* is the countryman, the peasant farmer and man of the soil, whom César Manrique considered to be the very backbone of every nation, and the foundation on which its history and culture stands.

The white Campesino Monument, which marks the centre of the island, is Manrique's tribute to the hard-working farming people of Lanzarote, who have long battled with the inhospitable terrain of their native island. Deeply moved by the labours that created the vineyards of La Geria (► 54–55), he dedicated the 15m-high (49ft) work, which stands prominently at a road junction outside the wine-producing village of Mozaga, 'to the forgotten endeavours of the unknown farmers of Lanzarote'.

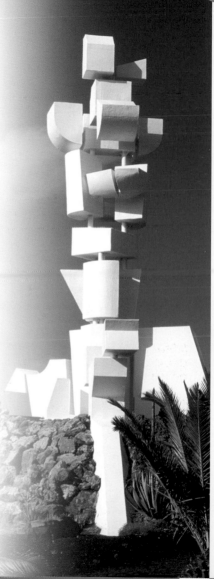

The enigmatic cubist monument was constructed in 1968 from farm debris, water tanks and old fishing boats, and is said to represent the farmer, his dog and a rat.

The Casa-Museo del Campesino is a copy of a fine traditional farm building and farmyard presented as a pristine black, white and green artwork. You can see an old preserved kitchen, tools and equipment, as well as a reproduction of a cottage workshop, although the main exhibit is the building itself. In keeping with Manrique's ideas, an attractive farm-style restaurant at the site serves lunch, with dishes from Lanzarote.

� 6C ✉ Between San Bartolomé and Mozaga ☎ 928 52 01 36 🕐 Daily 10–6 🎟 Free 🍴 Restaurant (€) 🕐 Daily 12–4:30 🚌 Nos 16 and 20 to Tinajo, La Santa and Sóo

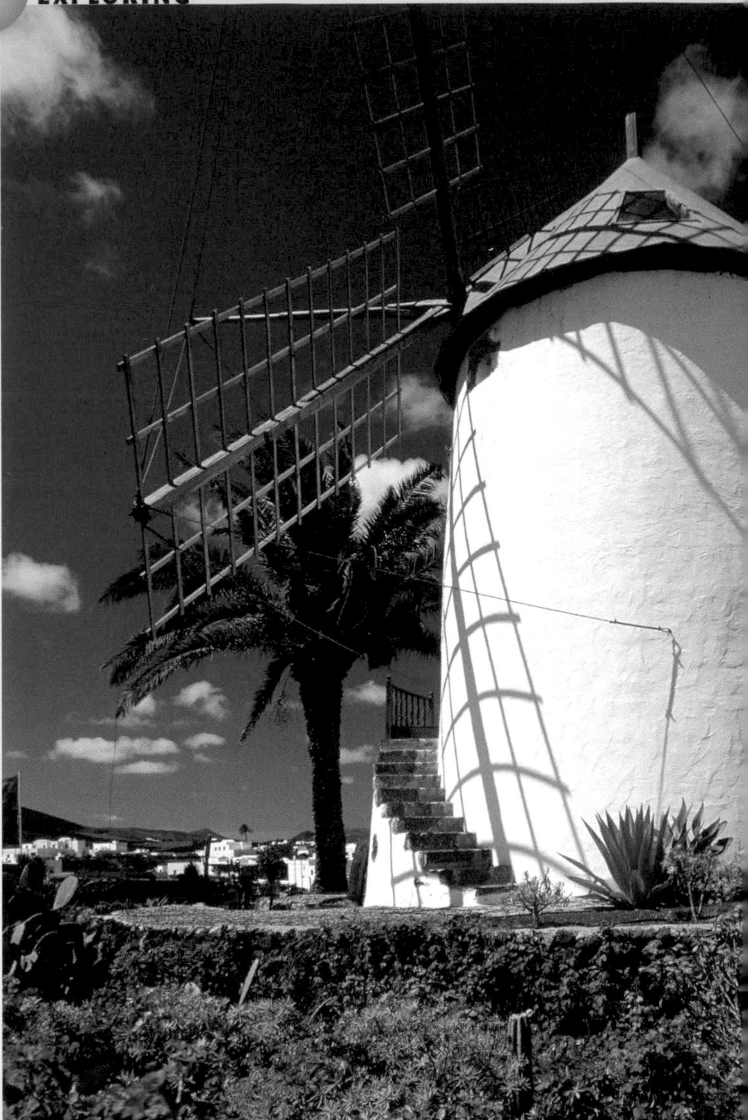

MUSEO AGRÍCOLA EL PATIO

In a suitably rural location at the centre of the island, this agricultural museum has exhibits on life in the countryside around 50 to 100 years ago and gives an opportunity to see and learn about Lanzarote's intriguing, ingenious and unusual farming traditions. More than a museum, this is a peaceful, immaculately restored traditional farm, dating from the 1840s. Visitors are guided around to take a close look inside one of the restored windmills and farm buildings, where goats, chickens and camels are bred. At the end of the tour there is the opportunity to taste the wines and goats' cheese produced on the estate.

www.museoelpatio.net

✚ 5B ✉ Just outside Tiagua on the road to Sóo ☎ 928 52 91 34 🕓 Mon–Fri 10–5:30, Sat 10–2:30. Closed Sun ✋ Inexpensive 🍴 Simple, pleasant bar (€) on site 🚌 No 13 (Arrecife–Sóo)

PAPAGAYO

Breezy Punta de Papagayo (Papagayo Point) and the more sheltered sandy bays either side of it lie at Lanzarote's southernmost tip. These are just about the finest beaches on the island: sweeps of fine golden sand edged by the clear waters of the channel separating Lanzarote from Fuerteventura. Thankfully, these excellent beaches can prove hard to find, and some still have to be reached on unmade roads with few, if any, signposts to guide the driver. Despite this, they do attract plenty of visitors, and they can get almost crowded at times.

The main beach, Playa de Papagayo (*papagayo* means parrot), is barely more than 15 minutes' drive from the resort town of Playa Blanca, much of it on dirt tracks. As the most easily accessible beach from Playa Blanca, from where water taxis operate (just continue a little way past Águila), it is also the most popular.

The ruined hamlet of El Papagayo, which is also signposted, is now home to sun-loving hippies. A string of other lovely beaches stretching around the peninsula of Punta de Papagayo, backed by sandy cliffs, are best reached on foot: Playa de los Pozos, Playa de Mujeres and, beyond the point, the nudists' secluded favourite, Playa de Puerto Muelas or La Caleta del Congrio. Be warned, however: none of these beaches has any shade or facilities, so bring a parasol, water and food, if needed.

All along this sandy stretch of coast, there are superb views to Fuerteventura – and from high points on the cliffs you can even see Puerto del Carmen and Arrecife. The Papagayo beaches now form a reserve to protect their unspoiled nature.

➕ 3F ✉ 6km (4 miles) east of Playa Blanca on the coast road; €3 fee for the car park at Playa de Papagayo 🚌 Nearest bus service is at Playa Blanca

a walk along the Tremesana Route

Unregulated walking is not permitted in Timanfaya National Park for fear of walkers injuring themselves, or damaging the fragile lichens that live on the volcanic rock. It has taken over 200 years for even this minimal flora to get established. There are two free guided walks in English supervised by the park authority (you must book in advance). This walk, the Tremesana Route, is easier than the Shore Route, which can be done unaccompanied. The Mancha Blanca Interpretation Centre provides a fascinating introduction to this region (➤ 134).

The walk starts or ends with a short minibus ride. From Yaiza, the group starts walking near the foot of Montaña Tremesana.

Here, figs are cultivated in stone half-circles to protect them from the wind.

Continue towards Caldera Rajada, ahead.

The volcano erupted from the side, splitting the mountain. Guides will point out amazing colours in the rocks, and explain how the eruption created tunnels underground (which can be seen at close quarters at Jameos del Agua). Tell-tale signs, such as yellow sulphur stains, show the guide where these occur.

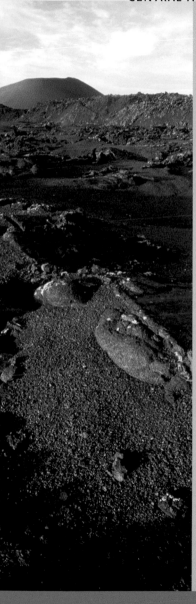

The route continues between two other volcanoes, Hernández and Encantada. Here you can see evidence of plant colonization.

The walk finishes at a track near the foot of a volcano called Pedro Pericó. Walkers are picked up by minibus and returned to the interpretation centre via Yaiza (➤ 150).

Distance 2km (1.2 miles)
Time 3 hours
Start/end point
Interpretation Centre ✚ 3C
Reservations ☎ 928 84
08 39. Walks take place on
Mon, Wed and Fri
Lunch Take a packed lunch

PARQUE NACIONAL DE TIMANFAYA
(TIMANFAYA NATIONAL PARK)

The otherworldly scenery of the park is often compared to a moonscape. Lichens are its only real inhabitants, forming colourful carpets on the inhospitable volcanic surface. If you are lucky, you may spot a visiting Egyptian vulture or Atlantic lizard. A stylized devil is the symbol of the park. With his horns, tail and trident, he conjures up a sense of mischief and fun, but while the Mountains of Fire may be fun to visit, they are a serious power. There are 36 volcanic cones within the park's 8sq km (3sq miles), including Islote de Hilario (➤ 44–45), and these volcanoes are still active. The grey desert of clinker and ash that surrounds the cones is the result of 26 eruptions between 1730 and 1736.

The start of those events was witnessed by the priest of Yaiza, Don Andrés Lorenzo Curbelo, who described them in his diary: 'On the first day of September 1730, between nine and ten at night, the earth suddenly opened close to Timanfaya, two leagues from Yaiza. During the first night an enormous mountain rose up from the bowels of the earth, with flames shooting from its summit, which continued burning for 19 days.'

A later entry in the diary recorded: 'On 18 October three new openings formed above Santa Catalina from which dense smoke emerged, which scattered over the entire island. The explosions which accompanied this phenomena, the darkness caused by the mass of grains and the smoke which covered the island, forced the inhabitants of Yaiza to flee their homes.'

Yaiza was lucky. Eleven other farming villages and hamlets were totally destroyed. Seventy years later, a series of earthquakes rocked the area again, culminating in the eruption of El Tinguatón volcano in 1824. The extraordinary terrain of Timanfaya, with its

volcanic tubes, cones and bubbles, was finally declared a national park in 1974.
✚ 3C

Echadero de los Camellos (Camel Park)

Lanzarote's camels are actually dromedaries, but nobody's quibbling over what is really just an amusement for tourists. The camel park is a corral at the foot of Timanfaya, where visitors can wait in line for a 10-minute ride up the steep, unstable slag heap of the volcano. Each animal carries two or three passengers, who are strapped into wooden seats, perched on either side of the camel. The camel train is then led up the slope by a guide.

✉ 3km (2 miles) north of Yaiza, at the foot of Timanfaya/Islote de Hilario (➤ 44–45) ☎ 928 04 08 39 ⏰ Daily 9–4 💷 Expensive 🍴 El Diablo restaurant (€€; ➤ 60) at the summit

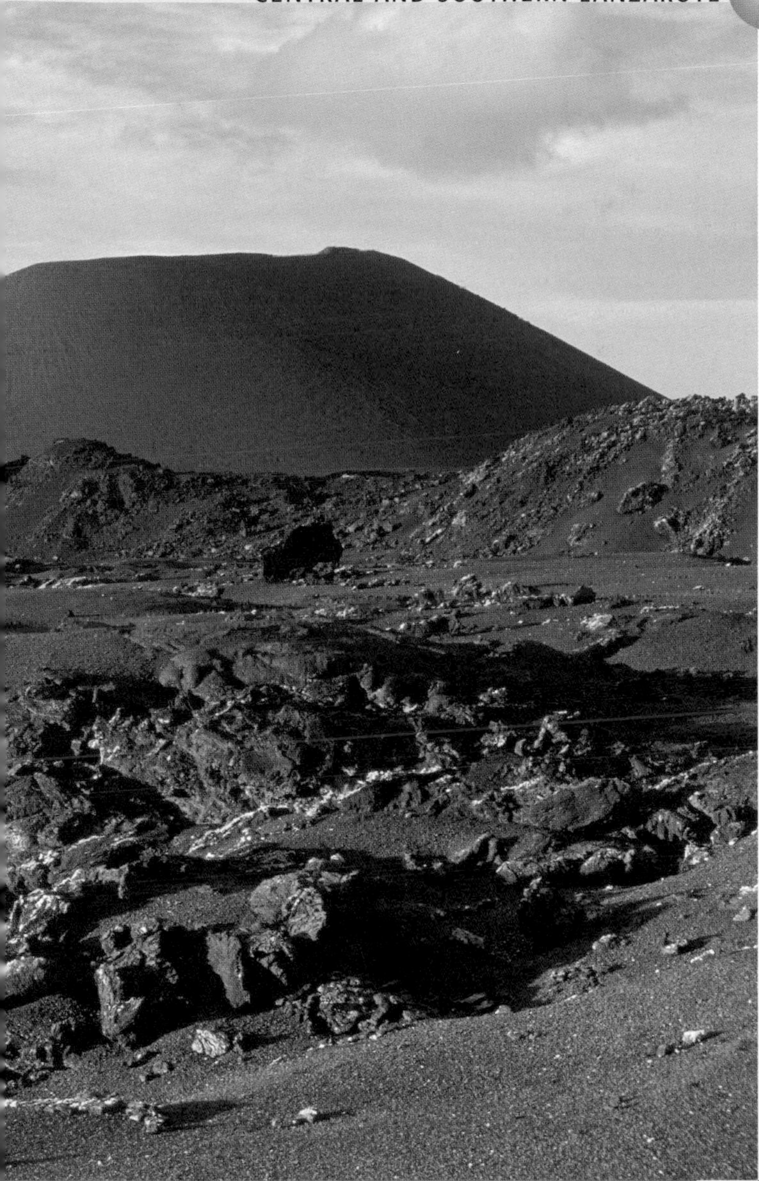

Mancha Blanca Centro de Visitantes e Interpretación

Situated on the park boundary, near the village of Mancha Blanca, the interpretation centre is one of the park's most interesting sights – and one of the few man-made items in the landscape. The building at first appears small and low, its whiteness a sharp contrast with the dark lava. However, it turns out to be much larger, with most of the centre lying underground. Inside, a cool, calm environment contains fascinating video and interactive exhibitions about the park, an accessible library and a bookshop, as well as viewpoints onto the volcanic terrain. Among the most interesting exhibits is the Eruption Hall, simulating the movements, noise and smoke at the time of the 1730 volcanic eruption here.

🕂 3C ✉ 9km (5.5 miles) from Islote de Hilario, at Mancha Blanca ☎ 928 84 08 39 🕒 Daily 9–5 ✋ Free 🍽 El Diablo restaurant (€€; ➤ 60) on the Islote de Hilario summit 🚍 None

Montaña Rajada

Only to be seen on the Ruta de los Volcanes bus tour, which starts from the Islote de Hilario summit, this 373m (1,224ft) peak gives one of the most awe-inspiring views of the park: a panoramic vista over volcanic cones and craters and the hollows caused by underground tunnels collapsing. Beyond, the blue sea makes a startling contrast.

🕂 3C ✉ 2km (1 mile) southwest of Islote de Hilario 🚍 On Ruta de los Volcanes bus tour

Montaña de Timanfaya

This, the largest of the park's volcanoes at 511m (1,676ft), is a vast dark cone that dominates the view throughout western Lanzarote. You can see it up close and admire the vivid red and yellow streaks (caused by mineral deposits) on the volcanoes coach tour.

✚ 3C ✉ 1km (0.5 miles) southwest of Islote de Hilario 🚌 On Ruta de los Volcanes bus tour

Playa de la Madera

Where the park meets the sea there are many inaccessible coves and black sand beaches. One, however, can be reached by car on a track that is marked – very truthfully – Camino en Mal Estado (track in poor condition). The track can be reached from Tinajo, Mancha Blanca or a turn close to the Islote de Hilario entrance.

✚ 3B ✉ 10km (6 miles) northwest of Mancha Blanca 🚌 None

Timanfaya Plain

The flat lowland that lies at the foot of the volcanoes is a sea of dark jagged rock, resembling coal cinders. The terrain is so unusual that it deserves a good look.

✉ Between Yaiza and park entrance

Valle de la Tranquilidad (Valley of Tranquillity)

In this part of the park some tiny bushes are trying to grow and a few tufts of grey-looking grasses manage to cling to the slopes, a hint of the future greenery that may one day take hold here.

✉ 1km (0.5 miles) south of Islote de Hilario 🚌 On Ruta de los Volcanes bus tour

PLAYA BLANCA

This purpose-built resort on the southern shore basks in a sheltered position where the wind and the waves are subdued.

The town's pleasant, golden sandy main beach catches the sun, is perfectly protected from the breeze, and is backed (in town) by an attractive promenade with plenty of greenery and café tables. There are two smaller beaches east of the centre, and another attractive beach area west of the port.

For now, Playa Blanca remains a quiet little place, with an away-from-it-all feeling that belies the fact that it is only 15km (9 miles) on a fast road across the Rubicón plain to Yaiza, and is therefore very conveniently placed for visiting Timanfaya National Park and the southern half of the island. It's also handy for the west coast, where the volcanic *malpaís* reaches down to the Atlantic breakers.

From Playa Blanca's seashore you can look across the 11km-wide (7 mile) channel to Fuerteventura and the small dark volcanic shape of Isla de Lobos. Ferries cross to Fuerteventura several times a day from Playa Blanca's main harbour for an easy and enjoyable day excursion. Fishing boats use the harbour too, and restaurants along the promenade feature plenty of freshly caught fish. There's also the increasingly popular Marina Rubicón, which has some shops and great waterside bars and restaurants.

The harbour area and the few streets to the east were the only part of Playa Blanca that existed before tourism took off. West of the harbour there is another development of shops, restaurants and accommodation, round a sheltered little bay of fine sand.

Playa Blanca is the furthest south of Lanzarote's resorts, a relatively long way from the sights in the north, but it has some clear advantages for those who want sun, sea and sand, good food and a peaceful atmosphere. With almost nothing here before the resort was built, it is dedicated to holiday enjoyment. Most entertainment is provided by the hotels, which in Playa Blanca are of a high standard. Set back from the promenade, attractive

holiday apartment complexes and imaginatively designed, good-quality modern hotels are just a few paces from the sea.

Many visitors search out the more secluded sandy beaches to both the east and west, including impressive Playa de Papagayo (➤ 126). To get your bearings, follow the coast round to the lonely clifftop Castillo de las Coloradas, which can be seen from anywhere in Playa Blanca. From here, in a beautiful sweep of coast, the great sandy bays of Papagayo can be glimpsed between the string of headlands that stretch to Punta de Papagayo. The easiest way to visit the more remote beaches is to rent a small boat from the harbour at Maga Blanca. Alternatively, you can take the coastal walkway from town either east to Playa de las Coloradas (2km/1mile) or west to the lighthouse at Punta Pechiguera (2km/1 mile), drive or take a taxi.

🚏 2F ✉ 35km (22 miles) from Arrecife 🍴 Bars and snack bars (€) and restaurants (€–€€) on the promenade 🚌 No 6 from Arrecife or Puerto del Carmen to Playa Blanca; frequent departures daily 🚢 To Corralejo, on Fuerteventura, several times a day. There are also ferries to Lobos Island, in between the two larger islands (➤ 26–27)

PUERTO CALERO

The island's most exclusive marina is the starting point for many catamaran and submarine trips. Puerto Calero is also worth a visit for its **Museo de Cetáceos** (Cetacean Museum). Interactive exhibits feature information on whales, porpoises and dolphins.

➕ 4E 🚌 No 2 six times a day to Puerto del Carmen and Arrecife

ℹ️ Avenida de las Playas ☎ 928 51 33 51

Museo de Cetáceos

✉️ Edificio Antiguo Varadero ☎ 928 84 95 60; www.museodecetaceos.org

🕐 Daily 10–6. Closed first Thu of each month ✋ Expensive (under 6 free)

PUERTO DEL CARMEN

Lanzarote's main resort is surprisingly small and low-key, yet it has 5km (3 miles) of broad pale sand beaches, a wide choice of places to eat and stay, and is an excellent base for reaching all the other sights of the island.

Puerto del Carmen is almost entirely a new town, a narrow strip clinging to the beach and dedicated to tourism. To the north it spreads out towards the airport and Arrecife, while at the other end of town lies the original fishing harbour. A coastal walkway links Puerto del Carmen with Arrecife. Running for 9km (5.5 miles) along the lovely beaches of Los Pocillos, Guasimeta and Honda, it can also be cycled, with the occasional detour.

➕ 5E

Old Harbour

The small fishing harbour just south of Playa Grande was the heart of the original Puerto del Carmen village. It's still very much in use today, and gives character to this part of town; in the square next to the port, you can watch the locals playing boules and enjoy excellent fresh fish in one of the nearby restaurants.

✉️ Western edge of town 🍴 Seafood restaurants (€–€€) surround the harbour 🚌 No 2 from Arrecife stops on Avenida de las Playas

Playa Grande (Playa Blanca)

The town's main beach, a delightful wide band of yellow sand, runs alongside busy Avenida de las Playas, the main artery of the town. Confusingly, it is often referred to as Playa Blanca, the same name as a quite separate resort at the southern tip of the island. On the beach side of the Avenida there's an attractive paved walkway with palm trees and gardens; across the street is a long strip of bars and restaurants, bright lights, tourist shops and places of entertainment. After dark, the Centro Atlántico along here is the

place to find clubs and nightlife. The promenade continues to Pocillos and Matagorda beaches, which makes a lovely walk.

➕ 5E 🍽 Restaurants (€€) on Avenida de las Playas 🚌 No 2 from Arrecife every 20 mins (30 mins Sat–Sun)

ℹ Avenida de las Playas

☎ 928 51 33 51

Playa de los Pocillos

With a vast, sandy beach 2km (1 mile) east of Puerto del Carmen, Pocillos is a much quieter and less crowded resort area, with some above-average accommodation. The northern end of Pocillos beach is an appealing stretch with good restaurants and shops, called Los Jameos Playa – also the name of an excellent hotel here.

➕ 6E 🍽 Restaurants (€) at CC Jameos Playa 🚌 Buses from Arrecife approx every 30 mins

Playa de Matagorda

About 4km (2.5 miles) from town along the promenade, Matagorda has few attractions and feels remote. However (apart from daytime aircraft noise) it is tranquil and traffic-free, with a section of sandy beach and a shopping centre.

➕ 6D 🍽 CC Matagorda (€) 🚌 No 2 every 20 mins (30 mins Sat–Sun) to Puerto del Carmen and Arrecife

a drive around southern Lanzarote

This trip takes in quiet inland areas, visiting vineyards and wineries. It also passes through an extraordinary landscape of pretty villages, a patchwork of saltpans and scenic beaches.

From the Arrecife city ring road (Circunvalación) take the turn to San Bartolomé (► 144). Stay on this rural road until you reach the junction with the road to Uga and Yaiza, on the left.

At this junction is Manrique's striking cubist monument to the *campesino*, or peasant and adjoining farm museum (► 122–123).

Take the Yaiza road. Beware – it is narrow, and passing can be difficult.

This road enters La Geria, where vines grow in hollows dug into volcanic desert. After 13km (8 miles) it reaches the attractive village of Uga (► 148–149).

At the junction at the other end of Uga, turn right for pretty Yaiza (► 150) which lies on the edge of the dark malpaís. Stop in the village for a walk and perhaps lunch.

Continue through Yaiza on the main Playa Blanca road. After some 3km (2 miles), on the right beside a junction, are the strange geometric salt pans of Janubio (► 109).

The road soon begins to cross the flat, rather bleak Rubicón plain. Follow it right into the resort of Playa Blanca (► 136–137).

Take a stroll along the promenade of this small, modern beach resort. For a bigger beach, and fewer people, explore Papagayo, down a coastal track east of town (➤ 126–127).

Take the less-frequented, minor road 6km (4 miles) northeast towards Femés (➤ 119). Continue another 6km (4 miles) to the main road and turn right for Puerto del Carmen.

The road winds steeply down into Puerto del Carmen (➤ 138–141), a lively, pleasant family resort, with a big beach backed by restaurants.

Take the main road past the airport and back into Arrecife.

Distance 70km (43 miles)
Time 5 hours
Start/end point Arrecife ✚ 7D
Lunch La Casona de Yaiza (€€€; ➤ 159)

SAN BARTOLOMÉ

This often overlooked country town, all in traditional black, white and green, has the simple style that César Manrique was fighting to preserve. In a grand old house down a side-street, the **Museo Etnográfico Tanit** displays the island's unique folk culture. Its eclectic assortment of photos, paintings, furniture, wine-making paraphenalia, tools, kitchenware and religious artefacts inspire admiration for the history and heritage of the local people. Behind the courtyard stands a tiny private chapel and a garden.

🚹 6C 🍴 Bars and pastry shop (€) 🚌 Several buses from Arrecife

Museo Etnográfico Tanit

✉ Calle Constitución ☎ 928 52 06 55; www.museotanit.com
🕐 Mon–Sat 10–2 ✋ Moderate

SALINAS DE JANUBIO

At several places around the island shallow sea-water lagoons have been transformed into salt pans. One of the first, and still the most productive of these saltworks, was the lagoon at Janubio, on the southern edge of Timanfaya National Park. The large salty lagoon has been divided into fascinating neat rectangles subdivided very precisely into hundreds of smaller squares. As the water evaporates, it changes colour and consistency, and ultimately dries away leaving large quantities of salt. Despite this very functional purpose, the salt pans look, like so much else on Lanzarote, as if they were intended primarily to be extraordinary works of art.

The salt is used in the island's traditional, and still important, fish processing and preserving industries.

🚹 2D ✉ Just off the main road from Yaiza to Playa Blanca, at the junction for El Golfo; several viewpoints

LA SANTA

La Santa is a popular little village in the middle of the wilder, less populous north coast, and is well placed for a lunch stop. It overlooks the curious low-lying peninsula known as La Isleta, which lies about 2km (1 mile) east of the village, cut off from the mainland only at very high tides. To reach the island, simply continue on the road past the entrance to Club La Santa.

Club La Santa, situated on La Isleta, is one of the world's top private residential sports resorts. Guests enjoy full access to the exclusive facilities that include several swimming pools, restaurants and an extensive programme of sports (➤ 153).

✚ 5A 🍴 Fresh-fish restaurants (€) in village 🚌 No 16 runs between Arrecife and La Santa 8 times a day Mon–Fri, 3–5 times a day Sat–Sun. It takes about an hour each way

UGA

An incongruously green and fertile wine village on the fringes of the desolate volcanic terrain of the Timanfaya National Park, Uga stands at the western end of the bizarre La Geria vineyard area, where the vines grow amongst volcanic rubble.

Despite the dramatic location, Uga's simple, single-storey, white dwellings give it a neat, rather African charm. One of its main enterprises is breeding camels: not only do the animals that

carry tourists up Islote de Hilario come from here, but also those that are used for safaris on the island.

To see the vineyards, drive out of Uga on the road to San Bartolomé via Mozaga, La Geria's main town and wine outlet. Be warned that in places the road becomes rough and very narrow.

✚ 3D ✉ 17km (10.5 miles) west of Arrecife 🚌 No 6 (Arrecife–Playa Blanca)

VALLE DE LA GERIA

Best places to see, ➤ 54–55.

YAIZA

This arty, unpretentious, picturesque old village of palm trees and dazzling whiteness may well be one of the prettiest villages in the Canary Islands. It is dramatically located between golden hills and barren blackness. Standing on the very edge of the *malpaís*, it was all

but destroyed in the Timanfaya volcanic eruptions of 1730–36. Just a handful of houses survived, but, as many surrounding fields and gardens were left intact, villagers gradually returned and rebuilt their homes.

The sunshine reflects brilliantly off the simple whitewashed walls and houses. Some of the homes look prosperous and dignified, with little balconies and pleasing, flower-filled gardens. César Manrique wanted the whole island to look like this.

While in the village, pop into the 18th-century church whose tower rises over the main square, Plaza de los Remedios, and visit the municipal art gallery at the Casa de Cultura or the Galería Yaiza art gallery. The latter exhibits local paintings and ceramics, and most of the work on show is for sale.

✚ 3D ✉ 15km (9 miles) from Playa Blanca, around 20km (12.5 miles) from Arrecife 🚌 No 6 runs frequently between Arrecife and Playa Blanca

HOTELS

ARRECIFE
Hotel Lancelot (€€)
Cool and comfortable, this moderately priced hotel has a strongly Spanish feel. It faces sandy Playa del Reducto beach, a 5-minute walk from the town centre.

✉ Avenida Mancomunidad 9 ☎ 928 80 50 99; www.hotellancelot.com

MASDACHE
Finca Malvasia (€€)
This beautiful, boutique-style guesthouse offers luxury apartments, each with its own terrace, set around a lagoon-like pool. There's no restaurant, but good, reasonably priced, breakfasts are available on request. The welcoming English hosts personally assist guests with recommendations on what to see and do.

✉ Camino el Oratorio 12–14, Masdache ☎ 928 17 34 60;
www.fincamalvasia.com

MOZAGA
Caserío de Mozaga (€€)
A brother and sister have turned their 18th-century ancestral home into a charming hotel in lovely grounds. This is an intimate, rural place to stay, which also has a very decent restaurant.

✉ Mozaga 8 ☎ 928 52 00 60; www.caseriodemozaga.com

PLAYA BLANCA
Casa de Embajador (€€€)
A former ambassador's residence dating from the 1900s, this is a delightful, small, family-run hotel in a beachside location. All rooms have stunning views across Fuerteventura and the Isla de Lobos. Despite its central position in the resort, the hotel is very tranquil. The lack of swimming pool and child-friendly facilities makes it more suitable for couples than families.

✉ Calle La Tegala 30 ☎ 928 51 91 91

Timanfaya Palace (€€€)

The spectacular white exterior of domes, turrets, timbers and openings is modelled on traditional local architecture, while a curved frontage *à la* Manrique arches towards the sea. The lavish interiors are cool, comfortable and stylish. The hotel has a narrow but pleasant sandy beach in front, lined by a walkway.

✉ Playa Blanca (Limones end) ☎ 928 51 76 76; www.h10.es

PUERTO DEL CARMEN

Beatriz Playa (€€€)

Adjacent to the beachfront promenade, this comfortable, popular, family-friendly hotel with poolside gardens and terraces is close to Matagorda's shops and restaurants. There is periodic noise from aircraft – the airport lies behind the hotel – but none at night.

✉ Urbanización Matagorda ☎ 928 51 21 66; www.beatrizhoteles.com

Club Hotel Riu Paraíso Lanzarote (€€€)

Hardly visible from the road, this elegant, comfortable, low-rise hotel is 30m (98ft) from Playa de los Pocillos. The extensive facilities include seven swimming pools, a health and beauty centre, gym, Jacuzzi and sauna. There are many bars and restaurants to choose from. All-inclusive stays only.

✉ Calle Suiza 6 ☎ 928 51 24 00; www.riu.com

Los Fariones (€€€)

One of the island's older hotels, Los Fariones stands in a privileged position between Puerto del Carmen's old harbour and its long sandy main beach. A civilized tranquillity pervades the hotel, and the pool area and shaded waterside terraces are delightful. The hotel's sheltered beach is ideal for children, while guests also have access to a well-equipped sports complex across the road.

✉ Calle Roque del Este 1 ☎ 928 51 01 75; www.grupofariones.com

Los Jameos Playa (€€€)

An impressive, luxurious hotel in the style of a grand Canarian mansion. Wooden galleries surround a central patio with a delightful setting, while the extensive palm-shaded outdoor terrace has swimming pools and an excellent restaurant. As well as great children's facilities, there are tennis courts and a spa, and nightly entertainment.

✉ Playa de los Pocillos ☎ 928 51 17 17; www.seaside-hotels.de

San Antonio (€€)

One of the original hotels on the island, the San Antonio stands in a quiet part of the resort, between Playa de los Pocillos and the main beach. Pleasant palm and cactus gardens and heated outdoor pools.

✉ Avenida de las Playas 84 ☎ 928 51 42 00; www.hotelsantonio.com

LA SANTA

Club La Santa (€€)

Near the village of La Santa, on the breezy north shore of the island, this is one of the most highly rated sports resorts in the world. The tremendous range of facilities and full programme of sports and sightseeing activities are reserved exclusively for guests staying at the resort. There are several swimming pools, including a 50m (164ft) one, four restaurants, a late-night disco, and extensive facilities for young children. Accommodation is in self-catering apartments and must be pre-booked.

✉ Club La Santa, Tinajo ☎ In Lanzarote: 928 59 99 99. In UK: 0161 790 9890; www.clublasanta.com

YAIZA

Finca de las Salinas (€€€)

This small inland hotel has plenty of rustic charm. It's cool and peaceful inside, with flagstone floors and a lounge with cane seats arranged around palm trees growing through an open 'ceiling'. It has its own vegetable gardens and a small farm with animals. There is also a gym, tennis court and swimming pool.

✉ Calle La Cuesta 17 ☎ 928 83 03 25; www.fincasalinas.com

RESTAURANTS

ARRECIFE
Castillo de San José (€€)
See page 76.

Hotel Lancelot (€€)
The restaurant of this pleasant hotel (➤ 151) facing Arrecife's sandy beach is open to the public for very reasonable international cooking.
✉ Avenida Mancomunidad 9 ☎ 928 80 50 99 ⏰ Lunch, dinner

Leito de Proa (€€)
Choose from mussels, paella, octopus or moray eel at this simple fish restaurant looking out onto the peaceful El Charco de San Ginés (➤ 112–113).
✉ Calle Ribera El Charco 2 ☎ 928 80 20 66 ⏰ 9:30am–midnight

LA ASOMADA
Bodega El Chupadero (€€)
See page 60.

EL GOLFO
Mar Azul (€–€€)
The terrace of the Azul is right on the water's edge, looking over the Atlantic breakers, and has an extensive menu of good fresh fish and seafood dishes. A very enjoyable place to eat.
✉ Avenida Marítima ☎ 928 17 31 32 ⏰ Lunch, dinner

Placido (€€)
Set right on the beach, this relaxed and likeable family-run restaurant focuses on fresh fish.
✉ Avenida Marítima 39 ☎ 928 17 33 02 ⏰ Lunch, dinner

MÁCHER
La Cabaña (€€)
This intimate restaurant with wonderful service is a real find, serving superb, imaginative cuisine. Starters such as duck salad

with ginger tend to have an Asian influence, but there are more traditional main courses. This place, run by an English couple, is popular so try to book ahead. It's a 10-minute taxi ride from Puerto del Carmen.

✉ 72, main road Arrecife to Uga, Mácher ☎ 650 685 662; www.lacabanamacher.com 🕐 Mon–Sat from 7pm

MOZAGA
Casa-Museo del Campesino (€€)
Beside the Campesino Monument and forming part of the museum (► 122), this attractive Manrique-built restaurant serves a wide range of traditional local dishes, with much use of *gofio*.

✉ San Bartolomé (on road between San Bartolomé and Mozaga) ☎ 928 52 01 36 🕐 Lunch

PARQUE NACIONAL DE TIMANFAYA
El Diablo (€€)
See page 60.

PLAYA BLANCA
El Almacén de la Sal (€€)
Right on the waterfront in a converted salt store – the wreck of a rowing boat hangs from the ceiling – this elegant, characterful place has a cool, attractive stone and timber interior. Or you can sit on the shaded terrace outside, under big parasols. The menu offers the best of fresh fish and meat dishes, and many local specialities.

✉ Paseo Marítimo 12 ☎ 928 51 78 85 🕐 Lunch, dinner (snacks all day); closed Tue

Brisa Marina (€€)
Half-way along the waterside walkway of the old part of the village, this popular place concentrates on tasty fresh fish and seafood. Service can be offhand.

✉ Avenida Marítima 24 ☎ 928 51 72 06 🕐 Lunch

Casa Roja (€€€)

This red-painted restaurant in Marina Rubicón is in a superb position, with attractive wooden terraces overlooking the water and a handsomely restored stone and wood interior. It specializes in fish and shellfish, such as seafood rice and tuna with roasted vegetables.

✉ Marina Rubicón ☎ 928 51 85 17 🕓 Lunch, dinner; closed Sun dinner

PUERTO CALERO
Amura (€€€)

If you fancy a splurge, this is the place to come. Choose between the minimalist and stylish interior or the waterside outdoor terrace, which has stunning views. The menu is nouvelle cuisine with local and Spanish influences. Dress to impress.

✉ Puerto Calero ☎ 928 51 31 81 🕓 Lunch, dinner; closed Mon

PUERTO DEL CARMEN
Bodegon (€)

This is a rare thing: a real Spanish restaurant in Puerto del Carmen. Around 50 types of tapas are served, along with fresh juices, cakes and spit-roast chicken. It does a great picnic takeaway.

✉ Calle Bajamar 17 ☎ 928 51 17 63 🕓 Lunch, dinner; closed Sun

La Cañada (€€)

A long-established restaurant just off Avenida de las Playas, serving delicious local and international dishes. One of the best in town.

✉ Calle César Manrique 2 ☎ 928 51 21 08 🕓 Lunch, dinner; closed Sun

Casa Siam (€€)

Authentic Thai cuisine and decor. This is the real deal and a welcome change from some of the eateries on the strip.

✉ CC La Penita, Avenida de la Playas ☎ 928 52 84 64 🕓 Dinner

Colón (€€€)

Elegant and tasteful restaurant with ornate tiles and pictures, offering impeccable service. Food is mainly French-style, ranging from fresh fish to the seven-course *menu gastronomique*. Wine buffs will be keen to treat themselves to something from the extensive wine list.

✉ CC Matagorda, Avenida de las Playas 47 ☎ 928 51 59 11
🕓 Lunch, dinner

Especiero (€€)

This enjoyable, good-quality, air-conditioned restaurant with spectacular sea views is a real find. Try one of the speciality flambé dishes, the tasty paella or something from the fixed-price menu.

✉ Avenida de las Playas 46 ☎ 928 51 21 82 🕓 Lunch, dinner

Lani's Grill (€€)

Good cooking and quick, polite service in several languages at this chain restaurant. With a rustic wood and ceramic interior, the grill offers a wide range of meat and fish dishes.

✉ Avenida de las Playas 5 ☎ 928 51 00 20 🕓 6pm–midnight

Lani's Terraza (€–€€)

Tiled floors, lots of leafy ferns, purple table-cloths and a little bit of mock Roman decor make this a pleasant setting for good, authentic Italian cooking. Very reasonable prices, particularly the set menu.

✉ Avenida de las Playas 41 ☎ 928 51 32 19 🕓 9am–11:30pm

La Lonja del Fondeadero (€–€€)

In the heart of the old port, this traditional, boisterous, quayside fried-fish bar has plain wooden tables around a central bar. Excellent fish at low prices, including paella.

✉ Calle Varadero ☎ 928 51 13 77 🕓 All day

El Molino (€–€€)

Elegant blue-and-white table-cloths and a sprinkling of Spanish specialities make this Pocillos beach restaurant a pleasant change from the rest. Good cooking and service at modest prices.

✉ CC Jameos Playa ☎ 928 51 28 87 🕓 All day

O Botafumeiro (€€)

This excellent seafood restaurant on Playa de los Pocillos is Spanish and French rather than Canarian in style.

✉ Alemania 7, CC Costa Luz, Avenida de las Playas ☎ 928 51 15 03
🕐 Lunch, dinner

El Orreo (€€)

Highly professional Galician cooking, attentive service and a great location make this one of the best beachside eateries, with excellent, good-value meat, fish and pasta. Good music.

✉ Avenida de las Playas ☎ 928 51 18 52 🕐 10am–11pm

Puerto Bahía

See page 76–77.

Terraza Playa (€€)

Steps decorated with black and white pebbles lead down to a beachside terrace under palm trees. This is a lovely spot, with good food and service, all reasonably priced.

✉ Avenida de las Playas 28 ☎ 928 51 54 17 🕐 Lunch, dinner

El Tomate (€€)

The popular 'Tomato' serves international food, while its sister restaurant, Tomatissimo, also along Calle los Jameos, specializes in Italian cuisine.

✉ Calle los Jameos ☎ 928 51 19 85 🕐 Dinner

Zaffran (€)

Excellent Indian food, prepared from the freshest ingredients, is served here. Friendly service, great atmosphere, reasonable prices and very cold beer make it popular. There's also a takeaway service.

✉ Olivin shopping centre, Calle Juan Carlos 1 ☎ 928 51 27 47 🕐 Dinner; closed Tue

LA SANTA
Los Charcones (€)
On the main road skirting the village, a couple of kilometres from Club La Santa sports resort (▶ 153), this unpretentious restaurant has a strongly Spanish feel and specializes in locally caught fish and seafood.

✉ Pueblo de la Santa 101, on the Tinajo road ☎ 928 84 03 27
🕐 Lunch, dinner

TIAGUA
El Tenique
A meal on one of the terraces at this village restaurant comes with a spectacular volcanic backdrop, as well as views of mountains and sea. Enjoy succulent grilled meats, delicious *sancocho* (fish stew) and local specialities, including goat stew on Sundays, and a consistently warm welcome.

✉ Arrecife–Tinajo road, Tiagua ☎ 928 52 98 56 🕐 Lunch, dinner; closed Tue

UGA
Casa Gregorio (€€)
A traditional Lanzarote inn serving the island's speciality dishes, including fried kid. On Sundays a traditional rich *puchero* stew is usually served.

✉ Calle Joaquín Rodriguez 15 ☎ 928 83 01 08 🕐 Lunch, dinner; closed Tue

YAIZA
La Casona de Yaiza (€€€)
A former winery, now a beautiful rural hotel and restaurant, the building stands sharply white against the volcanic La Geria setting.

✉ Calle El Rincón 11 ☎ 928 83 62 62; www.casonadeyaiza.com
🕐 Lunch Mon only, dinner Fri–Wed; closed Thu

SHOPPING

MARKETS

Saturday morning at El Charco de San Ginés, Arrecife, selling mostly clothes to locals.

Saturday morning at Tías. A small farmers' market selling local produce such as honey, cakes, organic fruit and vegetables, cheese and wine.

Wednesday and Saturday morning at Marina Rubicón, Playa Blanca (9am–2pm). A much smaller version of Teguise's market, selling souvenirs and local produce.

ENTERTAINMENT

CASINO

Casino de Lanzarote

Slot machines, blackjack and roulette tables, as well as a restaurant/bar. Over-18s only, with passport. However, there is a terrace with a bar with no age restrictions.

✉ Avenida de las Playas 12, Puerto del Carmen ☎ 928 51 50 00

🕓 Slot machines: 11am–4am. Bar and game hall: 5pm–4am. Bar and terrace: 9am–4am. Restaurant: 9pm–2am

DISCOS AND LATE-NIGHT BARS

All the resorts on both islands have late-night bars with music, but there are few real discos or dance venues. Those listed here open around 9 or 10pm (although they only really start filling up about midnight) and stay open until 2 or 4am.

Avenida de las Playas in Puerto del Carmen is Lanzarote's entertainment hub, and has a large number of late-night bars with live music and dancing. The focal point for most of the city's discos and nightclubs is Centro, the central section of the Avenida, about half-way along the main beach. Popular nightclubs here include César's. Café La Ola is part of a chain, but it's a stylish addition to the beach strip, with a fusion of Eastern and Moroccan decor, live music and performances.

In Arrecife, head to Calle José Antonio, a street with several nightspots open from midnight Wed–Sat. A little bit of Ibiza can be found at the new international lounge bar, Café del Mar, Marina Rubicón.

SPORTS

CYCLING
Ciclomania
Rental of mountain bikes for all ages. Children's seats also available.

✉ Calle Almirante Boado Endeiza 9 (opposite the Gran Hotel), Arrecife
☎ 928 81 75 35

DIVING AND SCUBA DIVING
Atlantica Diving Centre
Diving courses from the main beach for anyone over the age of 8.

✉ Aparthotel Fariones Playa, Calle Acatife 2, Puerto del Carmen
☎ 928 51 0/ 17; www.atlanticadiving.es

Cala Blanca Diving Centre
PADI courses for all levels. Guided dives, courses and equipment rental.

✉ CC El Papagayo 66, Playa Blanca ☎ 928 51 90 40;
www.calablancasub.com

Safari Diving
This PADI, professional centre for diving includes instruction and welcomes divers of all qualifications, as well as divers with disabilities, beginners, non-divers and children, for a wide range of courses. Organized dives include wreck, reef, cave and night diving.

✉ Playa de la Barrilla 4, Puerto del Carmen ☎ 928 51 19 92;
www.safaridiving.com

HORSE RIDING
Lanzarote a Caballo (Lanzarote on Horseback)
Horse riding in the Geria Valley, Playa Quemada or Playa Blanca, as well as riding lessons, camel rides and paintball combat. A children's adventure playground and restaurant are on site.

✉ On Arrecife–Yaiza road, close to Uga ☎ 928 83 00 38; www.lanzaroteacaballo.com

Rancho Texas Lanzarote
This western theme park set in attractive gardens offers pony rides, as well as falconry displays, animal enclosures and country-and-western evenings.

✉ Calle Noruega (signposted from Playa de los Pocillos beach), Puerto del Carmen ☎ 928 84 12 86; www.ranchotexaslanzarote.com ⏱ Daily 9:30–5:30

SPORTS CENTRE
Centro Deportivo Fariones
This sports centre, opposite Los Fariones hotel, has a heated swimming pool, gym, sauna and jacuzzi, as well as tennis and squash courts.

✉ Calle Roque del Este, Puerto del Carmen ☎ 928 51 47 90

WALKING
Canary Trekking
Guided volcano and nature park walks, including a visit inside a lava tunnel.

✉ Timanfaya ☎ 928 82 61 14; www.canarytrekking.com

ICONA National Parks Walking Service
Two guided walks in Timanfaya National Park (➤ 130–135), to a volcano or along the coast. The volcano one, The Tremesana Route (➤ 128–129) is the easier of the two. Groups are small and the emphasis is on the geology of the *malpaís* and its native species.

✉ Mancha Blanca Interpretation Centre, Timanfaya ☎ 928 84 08 39

Fuerteventura

A wild, unkempt, golden desert island of sunshine and sand, Fuerteventura looks like a fragment of the Sahara desert. Visitors exploring it will find light, peace, rocks of red and yellow and black, and wide open spaces. The sands have indeed blown here from the Sahara, on the strong winds that give the island its name.

Eastern Fuerteventura is sheltered, though even these coasts are famous for their windsurfing. In the interior and west, higher cones and ridges of darker rocks and vivid colours show the island's volcanic origin, though there hasn't been a murmur from these eroded volcanoes for thousands of years. Despite increasing tourism, there's a sense that little has changed here in a long time.

Corralejo

a drive around northern Fuerteventura

This drive passes through uninhabited areas of awe-inspiring emptiness, yet also fertile corners and picturesque villages with local handicrafts. The main roads are good, but there's nowhere to buy petrol, so take a full tank.

From Corralejo take the FV101 due south into the interior. After 7km (4 miles) turn right at the first turning, which goes to Lajares.

Lajares, a pretty village of white cottages, is noted for its embroidery and other traditional handicrafts.

Take the road to La Oliva, to a landscape of volcanic malpaís. On the left rises the soaring sandy mountain of Montaña Arena.

The village of La Oliva (➤ 175) brings together the island's history and its variety of imposing terrain.

Follow the road south, passing Montaña Tindaya on the right. Carry on to the junction at the foot of the dark volcano Montaña Quemada, 'Burnt Mountain'. The Unamuno memorial (➤ 174) can be seen from the road. Turn right towards Betancuria. At a T-junction, keep right across a plain, passing several windmills. Continue into hills, climbing up before winding sharply down into Betancuria.

Betancuria (➤ 166–167) has several interesting old buildings and deserves a leisurely stroll.

*Return up the steep hill road to take the turn for Antigua
(▶ 166), on the right. After exploring Antigua, visit the
restored windmills on the main road on the way north to
Puerto del Rosario (▶ 177). Turn onto the coast road
north towards Corralejo.*

The road crosses stony terrain for some 10km (6 miles)
before reaching El Jable, a thrilling landscape of pale dunes
designated as a Natural Park (▶ 40–41). Offshore is the
island of Lobos (▶ 172). The road continues into Corralejo.

Distance 115km (71 miles)
Time 4 hours
Start/end point Corralejo ✚ 17G
Lunch La Flor de Antigua (▶ 182)

ANTIGUA

Antigua dates back to 1485 and the early colonial period. Around the village much of Fuerteventura's historic character has been preserved. In the surrounding countryside windmills *(molinos)* still make use of the continual breezes to grind corn for *gofio*, the roasted, milled cereal that is a staple Canarian food. The 200-year-old El Molino, on the main road heading north from the village, has

been restored and converted into a delightful cultural and crafts centre, the **Centro de Artesanía Molino de Antigua,** with a craft shop, garden with palm and cactus, and galleries housing temporary exhibitions.

🕇 16M ✉ 21km (13 miles) southwest of Puerto del Rosario 🍽 La Flor de Antigua

(€€; ► 182) 🚌 No 1 from Puerto del Rosario to Morro Jable 6 times a day 🛈 Fiesta of Our Lady of Antigua, 8 Sep

Centro de Artesanía Molino de Antigua

☎ 928 87 80 41 🕐 Tue–Sat 9:30–5:30 ✋ Inexpensive

BETANCURIA

Named after the 15th-century Norman conqueror of this island, Jean de Béthencourt – Juan de Betancuría in Spanish – this bright, white village in the very centre of Fuerteventura remained its capital until 1834. Betancuria still keeps something of its historic, aristocratic character. De Béthencourt built his capital here in the belief that being so far from the sea, it would be safe from the Moorish pirates who terrorized the coasts. He was proved wrong; pirates repeatedly sacked the town, in 1593 destroying the original Norman-style cathedral and taking away 600 captives as slaves.

The church was rebuilt in 1620, in an interesting hybrid style, with a painted ceiling, a fine baroque altarpiece and ancient gravestones forming part of the floor. It became a cathedral again in 1924. Many village houses still have facades and doorways

dating from the 1500s and
1600s. Across the church
square, a museum devoted to
religious art displays de
Béthencourt's original
standard, the Pendón de la
Conquista. A **Museo Arqueológico y Etnográfico** (Museum of
Archaeology and Ethnography), across the (usually dry) river,
houses Guanche relics and local fertility symbols.

➕ 15M ✉ 28km (17 miles) southwest of Puerto del Rosario 🍴 Simple bar-
restaurant (€) beside Casa Museo; Restaurant Casa de Santa María (€€€), by
church 🚌 No 2 from Puerto del Rosario to Vega de Río Palma, twice a day
Mon–Sat

Museo Arqueológico y Etnográfico

✉ Calle Roberto Roldán 12–14 ☎ 928 87 02 41 🕐 Tue–Sat 10–5, Sun 11–2
✋ Inexpensive

CALETA DE FUSTE

This popular, fast-growing resort receives large numbers of package tourists in mainly budget accommodation, having the advantage (or disadvantage) of being close to the airport. Several mid-quality small hotels and low-rise budget apartments have been built here recently and more are going up. There's a very good golden beach, a few lively bars and several inexpensive eating places. An 18th-century fortified round tower of dark stone, called simply El Castillo – the castle – stands next to a marina and has become part of a beach complex with restaurant, bars, watersports rental facilities, and a supermarket.

🕂 17M ✉ 12km (7.5 miles) south of Puerto del Rosario
🚌 No 3 from Puerto del Rosario to Caleta de Fuste, via airport every 30 mins Mon–Sat, every hour on Sun

CORRALEJO

Though still a working fishing harbour and a pleasant small town, this is Fuerteventura's biggest and most accessible beach resort. Lying on the breezy northern tip of the island, just across the narrow strait from tourist developments on the southern tip of Lanzarote, Corralejo has woken up to the fact that it too has that magic formula sun, sea and sand. As a consequence, several hotels and apartment complexes have opened. For sun, its record can hardly be matched anywhere else in the Canaries. When it comes to sand, although the white beach in town is not very large, immense golden beaches and mountainous dunes stretch out just behind the town and go on for miles (➤ 41). The heart of the town centres on a bustling square with shops, bars and budget restaurants, and there is a more lively nightlife than in other resorts on Fuerteventura.

✚ 17G ✉ 30km (18 miles) north of Puerto del Rosario 🍴 Cafés and restaurants on beachfront (€–€€) 🚌 No 6 via Puerto del Rosario, every 30 mins Mon–Fri, hourly Sat–Sun ⛴ To Isla de Lobos (10 mins, Ferry Majorero ☎ 928 86 62 38); to Playa Blanca on Lanzarote (20 mins one way, Fred Olsen Line ☎ 928 53 50 90) ℹ Plaza Pública ☎ 928 86 62 35

EL COTILLO

This small holiday development around a fishing harbour on the windy west coast near La Oliva has black cliffs, sandy beaches,

watersports and an 18th-century fortification called the Torre del Tostón or Castillo de Rico Roque, which has been restored and contains a small art gallery. There's an away-from-it-all feeling. Windsurfers like the wild waves at the southern beach; families and sunbathers prefer the gentler northern beach.

➕ 15H ✉ 20km (12 miles) south of Corralejo 🍴 Fish restaurants (€–€€) on the harbour 🚌 No 8 to Corralejo every 2 hours Mon–Sat; No 7 three times a day Mon–Sat to Puerto del Rosario

ERMITA DE NUESTRA SEÑORA DE LA PEÑA

Tucked away in the hills outside Vega de Río Palmas, just south of Betancuria, is this remote, whitewashed hermitage. It's hard to reach, and getting there involves some stiff walking. The tiny building houses an alabaster statue of the revered patron saint of Fuerteventura. The third Saturday in September is her feast day, which brings crowds of islanders here for the all-important romería, a fascinating annual pilgrimage and procession.

➕ 14N ✉ 5km (3 miles) south of Betancuria on the Pájara road 🕐 Tue–Sun 11–1, 5–7. Closed Mon 🚌 No 2 from Puerto del Rosario to Vega de Río Palma twice a day

GRAN TARAJAL

Tarajal is the Canary tamarisk, numbers of which give a green aspect to this area and the valley of Gran Tarajal behind. Here, on a south-facing shore, dark hills reach the sea at this small, charmless harbour village, which claims to be Fuerteventura's second-largest town. Unusually for the island, the beaches have black sand. As well as tamarisk, the valley is noted for its date palms, which produce not only fruit, but also the raw materials for the island's ubiquitous straw hats and basketwork. Las Playas (or Las Playitas), a short drive up the coast, is another growing new development.

🚼 15Q 📧 45km (28 miles) south of Puerto del Rosario 🍴 Cafés and restaurants (€–€€) on the beachfront 🚌 No 1 from Puerto del Rosario to Morro Jable stops here, about 6 times a day ❓ Candlemas, on 2 Feb, is a big fiesta here, celebrated as the Fiesta de Nuestra Señora de la Candelaria

ISLA DE LOBOS

Lying some 3km (2 miles) from Corralejo, the tiny Island of the Seals – as its name literally means – is a haunting miniature world, a curious landscape of tiny volcanic protrusions rising from stones and sand. It is uncertain whether the island was named after real seals, as some claim, as there are no seals here now. Perhaps instead the *lobos* were the little rock mounds, which from afar do look like animals lying on a beach. The once-volcanic Montaña La Caldera, just 127m (416ft) high, rises above the rest. The island is a nature park and, despite being a popular boat outing for tourists, has no roads, no vehicles and few inhabitants, and so remains an unspoiled haven of calm and simplicity (➤ 68–69).

🔢 18G ✉ 3km (2 miles) from Corralejo 🍴 Bring refreshments with you
🚢 Ferries from Corralejo (➤ 169)

JANDÍA PENINSULA

In the south, Fuerteventura narrows at the sandy Pared Isthmus, before widening again to form the Jandía Peninsula, originally a separate island. A land of big skies and vast beaches, the peninsula is overlooked by Fuerteventura's loftiest peak, the 812m-high (2,664ft) extinct Pico de Zarza volcano (also known – you'll understand why as soon as you see it – as Orejas de Asno, 'donkey ears'). All around the steep upland there are long, wide swathes of pale sand and immense unspoiled beaches.

On the peninsula's eastern shore, Playa de Sotavento, or simply Sotavento, has 28km (17 miles) of sand. It's the site of the annual World Windsurfing Championships, though what makes this a windsurfer's and kitesurfer's heaven is being protected from the worst of the prevailing winds (sotavento means 'leeward'). The growing Costa Calma development lies at one end of the beach.

South of Sotavento, the coast turns sharply west to the unsightly developments around Jandía Playa resort and to Morro Jable, the peninsula's main town, which has a pleasant promenade, bars and restaurants, and a harbour. Beyond, the extreme tip of the island is edged with beautiful secluded bays.

On the western side, the broad golden sandy sweep of Playa de Cofete and Playa de Barlovento ('windward') are beautiful but windy, with powerful undercurrents that are dangerous for swimmers. Inland, close to the shacks of Cofete, is the isolated mansion of Herr Gustav Winter, the enigmatic German owner of the whole Jandía Peninsula during and after World War II. Stories abound about Winter (who was given the land by General Franco), his guests and his relations with the German, Spanish and Latin American dictatorships.

17S 80km (49 miles) south of Puerto del Rosario At Morro Jable, numerous eateries (€–€€) on the promenade No 1 from Puerto del Rosario to Morro Jable via all the resorts and beach stops of eastern Jandía (6 times a day); No 10 is an express service between Morro Jable and Puerto del Rosario via the airport, Caleta de Fuste, Gran Tarajal and Costa Calma; No 5 runs up and down the coast between Costa Calma and Morro Jable about every hour from 9:30–9:30 A regular jetfoil service connects Morro Jable with the islands of Gran Canaria and Tenerife (➤ 27) Local fiestas on the Jandía Peninsula include 16 Jul at Morro Jable, and the last Sat in Jul at La Pared CC de Jandía, Avenida Saladar, Morro Jable ☎ 928 54 07 76

MONUMENTO A DON MIGUEL DE UNAMUNO

At the foot of the volcanic Montaña Quemada, a monument records the exile to Fuerteventura of Miguel de Unamuno (1864–1936), the poet and thinker. While rector of Salamanca University, he made no secret of his republican views and openly criticized the monarchy. Banished here in 1924 for his political views, he fell in love with the island's landscapes and lifestyle. After only four months, de Unamuno returned to Europe and resumed his cosmopolitan life, yet despite his short time on the island, in letters and poems he often extolled the virtues of Fuerteventura's simple life (► 177).

➕ 16K ✉ Near the junction of Route 600 (the road to Corralejo via La Oliva) and Route 610 (the road from Puerto del Rosario to Betancuria) 🚌 No 2 (Puerto del Rosario to Vega de Río Palma)

LA OLIVA

Built in the early 17th century as a residence for Fuerteventura's military governors, this small town was the island's seat of government until 1880. Several fine old mansions survive from those days, though some are now derelict. The grandest of them is the long white La Casa de los Coroneles (the Colonels' House) or La Casa de la Marquesa, dating from 1650 and once belonging to the Cabrera Béthencourt family – their family crest can be seen above the entrance. Opposite is the surprising and enjoyable **Centro de Arte Canario,** which showcases modern art from the islands. **Casa de la Cilla,** also known as the Museo del Grano (Grain Museum), is housed in a granary

dating from the early 19th century and has an exhibition on the different grains grown in Fuerteventura.

On the road to Villaverde, windmills are a reminder that this area was a centre for production of *gofio*. North of the town rises sandy 421m-high (1,381ft) Montaña Arena.

🔁 17J ✉ 17km (10.5 miles) south of Corralejo 🍽 Cafés in village (€)
🚌 No 7 (Puerto del Rosario to El Cotillo) stops here 3 times a day each way Mon–Sat ❓ Fiesta of Our Lady of Candelaria, 2 Feb

Centro de Arte Canario
☎ 928 86 82 33 🕐 Mon–Sat 10:30–2 💷 Inexpensive

Casa de la Cilla, Museo del Grano
☎ 928 86 87 29 🕐 Tue–Fri, Sun 9:30–5:30 💷 Inexpensive

PÁJARA

The parish church of Nuestra Señora de la Regla at Pájara, in the island's western hills, is architecturally one of Fuerteventura's most important historic buildings. Built in sections – a roof beam in the presbytery is marked with the date 1687 – it has an altar that lovers of the baroque style will appreciate. The fascinating decorations above the doors on the pink sandstone main porch are much older, and in a style believed to have been inspired by contact with the Aztecs. The village itself is shady and enticing, a rustic farming community in a pleasant fertile setting.

🚻 14N ✉ 40km (25 miles) southwest of Puerto del Rosario 🍴 Bars (€) in the village 🚌 No 4 from Jandía once a day

PARQUE NATURAL DE LAS DUNAS DE CORRALEJO (DUNES OF FUERTEVENTURA)

Best places to see, ➤ 40–41.

PUERTO DEL ROSARIO

Nothing stood on this spot until the early 19th century, and until as recently as 1956 this unprepossessing town and harbour still went under its original name of Puerto Cabras ('Goat Port'). This seemed rather undignified for a capital city, so the grander and prettier name

Puerto del Rosario was adopted. It became Fuerteventura's main administrative centre in 1860. Today the harbour is the most important on the island, and around 50 per cent of Fuerteventura's population live here. Its only visitor attraction is the **Casa Museo Miguel de Unamuno,** devoted to the island's renowned poet exile (➤ 174).

Located beside the main church, this is the house where he lived during his enforced stay in the 1920s. As well as displaying pictures and artefacts about the writer, the house has been faithfully restored.

➕ 17L ✉ 30km (18 miles) south of Corralejo 🍴 Café-bars (€) near harbour 🚌 Depot for all bus routes ⛴ Trasmediterránea (☎ 928 85 08 77; www.trasmediterranea.es) operates ferries to Arrecife (Lanzarote) ✈ Flights to and from Arrecife (Lanzarote) on Binter Canarias (☎ 902 39 13 92; www.binternet.com)

❓ Fiesta of Our Lady del Rosario, 7 Oct

ℹ Avenida Constitución 5 ☎ 928 53 08 44

Casa Museo Miguel de Unamuno

✉ Virgen del Rosario 7 ☎ 928 86 23 76 🕐 Mon–Fri 9–2 ✋ Free

TEFÍA

At this tiny village, the **Ecomuseo de la Alcogida de Tefía** is a living museum of restored traditional houses where you can watch artisans making traditional handicrafts, and see farmyard animals. At nearby Tiscamanita, the **Centro de Interpretación de los Molinos** examines the vital role of windmills in the life of the island.

➕ 16K

Ecomuseo de la Alcogida de Tefía
☎ 928 17 54 34 🕐 Tue–Sat 10–6
 Moderate

Centro de Interpretación del los Molinos
☎ 928 16 42 75 🕐 Tue–Sat 10–6
✋ Inexpensive

TUINEJE

At the heart of the island and rather remote, this village – noted for its goat's cheese and tomatoes that are grown in *fincas* all around the town – keeps its ancient Moorish appearance. The altarpiece of the parish church has paintings of the Battle of Tamacita, when locals defeated English pirates. This event is commemorated annually on 13 October.

➕ 15P ✉ 32km (20 miles) south of Puerto del Rosario 🚌 No 1 (Puerto del Rosario to Morro Jable)

HOTELS

CALETA DE FUSTE
Barceló Club El Castillo (€€)

One of many low-rise, inexpensive aparthotel complexes, this hotel offers beachside accommodation in one- or two-storey, self-catering bungalows, with sea views and TV. Facilities include restaurants, bars, a disco, TV room, games room, swimming pools, Jacuzzi and a children's playground. There is day and evening entertainment for both adults and children, and guests receive a discount on use of the thalassotherapy centre in the neighbouring Barceló hotel.

✉ Caleta de Fuste ☎ 928 16 31 01; from UK 0845 090 3071; www.barceloclubelcastillo.com

Broncemar Beach (€)

This agreeable complex has 184 self-contained villas in a tropical garden setting with palms and greenery, close to the beach. Each villa is effectively a hotel room with its own kitchenette, TV and terrace. Attractive pool and sunbathing area.

✉ Calle Ajicán 4 ☎ 928 16 39 33; www.broncemar-beach.com

Elba Palace Golf (€€€)

This luxurious hotel is built in a traditional Canarian style, with wooden balconies and a plant-filled inner patio. Situated within a golf club, the hotel has two heated swimming pools, tennis courts, a gym, sauna and jacuzzi.

✉ Urbanización Fuerteventura Golf Club, Carretera de Jandía, Caleta de Fuste ☎ 928 16 39 22; www.hoteleselba.com

CORRALEJO
Club Hotel Riu Oliva Beach Resort (€€)

A comfortable, well-placed family hotel with small rooms but good access to the vast, beautiful beach, a swimming and sunbathing area, and an all-day's children's club. All-inclusive only.

✉ Avenida Grandes Playas (5km/3 miles south of town) ☎ 928 53 53 34; www.riu.com

Los Delfines (€)

This simple, white, two-storey complex of small self-catering apartments, each with its own terrace, is attractively arranged around a pool area. The complex has a TV room, supermarket and a buffet restaurant. Situated on the edge of Corralejo, some 200m (220yds) from the beach.

✉ Calle El Pozo 3 ☎ 928 53 51 43

Lobos Bahaí Club Aparthotel (€€)

An attractive pool complex and bar are at the heart of this better-than-average aparthotel, 800m (0.5 miles) from the beach. All one- and two-bedroom apartments have a kitchen area, balcony or terrace, and facilities include bars, restaurants, sports and entertainment programmes, TV room, games rooms, gym and more, as well as a small supermarket.

✉ Calle Gran Canaria 2 ☎ 928 86 71 43; www.lobosbahiaclub.com

Riu Palace Tres Islas (€€€)

On a wonderful location right next to the dunes, this stylish, comfortable and well-equipped 365-room hotel is ideally placed for exploring the north of the island. Luxurious bedrooms and private terraces overlook either the sea or the dunes, and there's a lovely pool and sunbathing area.

✉ Avenida Grandes Playas (5km/3 miles south of town) ☎ 928 53 57 00; www.riu.com

COSTA CALMA
Risco del Gato Suite Hotel (€€€)

One of the pioneers of the south, Risco del Gato is today jostled by its high-rise neighbour, but remains unequalled in style and class. Within its beautifully landscaped gardens are 51 suites housed in pod-like bungalows, each with a sea view, its own luxury bathroom and private sun terrace. There is also a spa, gym and gourmet restaurant.

✉ Calle Sicasumbre 2 ☎ 928 54 71 75; www.hotelriscodelgato.com

JANDÍA
Iberostar Palace (€€–€€€)
Situated on a 25km-long (15-mile) beach, this enormous, four-star hotel is just outside Jandía. It has an extensive pool complex that includes a jacuzzi and children's and heated pools, bars, restaurants, a dive centre and an entertainment programme.

✉ Los Gaviotas ☎ 928 54 04 44; www.iberostar.com

Melía Gorriones (€€€)
Renovated hotel in a beautiful, isolated position right on Sotavento beach, with pools, sun terraces and gardens. Excellent facilities include a health centre, gym, tennis courts and the famous Rene Egli windsurfing school (► 187).

✉ Playa Barca, Costa Calma ☎ 928 54 70 00, from UK 0800 962 720; www.somelia.com

PÁJARA
Hotel Rural Casa Isaítas (€€)
Housed in a stone building dating from 1890, this is a tranquil, friendly hotel with just four rooms, all furnished in an attractive rural style, with a library and a great restaurant.

✉ Calle Guize 7 ☎ 928 16 14 02; www.casaisaitas.com

RESTAURANTS

ANTIGUA
El Molino (€€)
It feels almost as if you are stepping inside a huge windmill as you enter this round building, which is in fact a beautifully restored former granary. The food is upmarket traditional Canarian cuisine.

✉ Carretera de Antigua Km 20 ☎ 928 87 85 77 🕒 Daily 10–6

La Flor de Antigua (€€)
Eat hearty home-cooking, grilled meat and fish, or classic Canarian fare at a spacious and lively eatery on the Betancuria road.

✉ Carretera General de Betancuria 43 ☎ 928 87 81 68 🕒 Lunch, dinner; closed Sun

BETANCURIA
Casa Santa María (€€–€€€)
See page 61.

Don Antonio (€€€)
In a rustic setting south of Betancuria, this appealing bar and restaurant has plenty of local atmosphere and a nice terrace where you can enjoy excellent Canarian cooking.

✉ Plaza de la Peña, Vega de Río Palma ☎ 928 87 87 57 🕐 Daily 10–5; closed Mon

CALETA DE FUSTE
Mona Lisa (€)
Good, varied menu of national and international dishes, huge pizzas and salads, and friendly service. A good place to take the children.

✉ Alcalde Juan Évora Suárez ☎ 928 16 34 26 🕐 Lunch, dinner

CORRALEJO
Bodeguita El Andaluz (€–€€)
Book ahead as this friendly, intimate restaurant is very popular. Excellent Spanish and international cuisine, and some wonderfully rich desserts.

✉ Calle La Ballena 6 ☎ 676 70 58 78 🕐 Dinner only

Chablis Wine Bar (€)
Friendly pub-restaurant with all your favourite hearty British dishes – but without the intrusions of TV, karaoke or thumping music. In the centre of town, the Chablis serves full English breakfast, lunch and dinner in relaxed surroundings. Try the breakfast or the roast dinner on Sunday nights.

✉ Corner Calle Anzuelo and Avenida Franco ☎ 928 53 52 91 🕐 9:30–2, 7– late (no food Sat pm or Wed am)

La Marquesina (€€)
See page 61.

Il Mulino (€–€€)

Authentic Italian cooking under a wooden arcade in a tiled alley by the harbour. Numerous meat and non-meat sauces to accompany fresh home-made pasta.

✉ Calle García Escámez 16 ☎ 928 86 71 05 🕓 6am–midnight

Rosie O'Grady's (€)

The best Irish bar in town, probably on the island. Live music every night and home-cooked food.

✉ Pizarro 10, off Calle de Lepanto, four blocks back from the High Street
☎ 928 86 75 63 🕓 After 7pm

El Sombrero (€€)

Mock-rustic decor and a touch of style distinguish this good Mexican restaurant. Specializing in steaks and fondues, and situated right on the harbourfront, you can enjoy your meal indoors or outside by the water.

✉ Avenida Marítima 17 ☎ 928 86 75 31 🕓 Dinner; closed Wed

El Tren (€–€€)

Enjoy fresh fish and seafood dishes at this restaurant in the heart of the town's harbourfront area, with a terrace overlooking the sea.

✉ Paseo Marítimo 12 ☎ 928 53 70 93 🕓 Lunch, dinner

Sotavento (€€)

Posters of the different kinds of fish and crustaceans help diners choose from an extensive seafood menu. Chops and steaks are also available. Smaller portions for children.

✉ 7 Avenida Marítima ☎ 928 53 64 17 🕓 Lunch, dinner

COSTA CALMA

Fuerte Action (€–€€)

Hang out with the local surfers and beautiful people at this friendly and relaxed trendy café. Lots of home-made dishes on the menu, including burgers, ice-cream and cakes, also good breakfasts and *tapas*. There's a terrace outside.

✉ CC El Palmeral (on main road next to the petrol station) ☎ 928 87 59 96
🕓 Daily 8am–12:30pm

EL COTILLO
La Vaca Azul (€€)
See page 61.

PÁJARA
Casa Isaítas (€€)
The true taste of Majorero home cooking can be sampled at this delightful rural hotel (➤ 182), which also opens to non-guests. The menu is extensive, with a good selection of vegetarian dishes.

✉ Calle Guize 7 ☎ 928 16 14 02 🕓 Mon–Wed 10–5, Sat–Sun 7am–9:30pm

PUERTO DEL ROSARIO
Antiguo (€€€)
One of the island's best restaurants, located in Hotel Fuerteventura, but open to the public, the Antiguo offers a reliable menu of Spanish and international flavours.

✉ Hotel Fuerteventura, Playa Blanca 45 ☎ 928 85 11 50 🕓 Lunch, dinner

Casa del Jamón (€€)
Some 5km (3 miles) west of Puerto del Rosario is this excellent family-run shop-cum-restaurant, which specializes in wine and *jamón* (cured ham). Typical Canarian fare is served, plus dishes from the Navarra and Basque regions. Extensive wine list.

✉ La Asomada (signposted off the main Tetir-La Oliva road and off the Carretera del Sur) ☎ 928 53 00 64 🕓 Daily 1–4pm

ENTERTAINMENT

DISCOS/LATE-NIGHT BARS
Blue Rock
Small bar playing rock and blues music, with an outdoor terrace.

✉ Calle Iglesia, just off the front, to the right of the tourist office, Corralejo
🕓 Thu–Tue 1pm–late; closed Wed

Rock Island
Friendly bar with regular live acoustic music. Extensive cocktail list.

✉ Calle Crucero Baleares 8, Corralejo ☎ 928 53 53 46;
www.rockislandbar.com 🕓 Daily 8pm–1am

SPORTS

BIG-GAME FISHING
Pez Velero
Deep-sea fishing trips leave from the harbour daily, by arrangement.

✉ Casa Mar y Juan, Pesca Deportiva, Calle Caravela 6, Corralejo
☎ 928 86 61 73 💷 Expensive (includes food and drink)

DIVING
Dive Center Corralejo
Morning dives at various locations, plus a 'bubblemaker' for 8- to 11-year-olds.

✉ Calle Nuestra Señora del Pino 22, Corralejo ☎ 928 53 59 06;
www.divecentercorralejo.com 🕒 Mon–Sat; closed Sun

SURFING
Ineika Funcenter
Rents boards and wetsuits, and offers full instruction for all levels.

✉ Ineika Apartamentos 53, Corralejo ☎ 928 53 57 44; www.ineika.de

Natural Surf Camp
✉ Calle La Mareta 3, Lajares ☎ 616 59 68 27; www.naturalsurfcamp.com

WALKING
Hannelore von der Twer
Knowledgeable guide offers coastal and volcanic nature walks.

✉ Villa Volcana, Villaverde ☎ 928 86 86 90, 608 92 83 80;
www.sports.fuerteonline.net

WINDSURFING, SURFING AND KITESURFING
Center René Egli
Equipment for hire and instruction on offers for all levels.

✉ Sol Gorriones Hotel, Playa Barca ☎ 928 54 74 83; www.rene-egli.com

Flag Beach Windsurf, Surf and Kitesurf Centre
Multi-lingual instructors and a beginner's 'teaching' lagoon.

✉ General Linares 31, Corralejo ☎ 928 86 63 89; www.flagbeach.com

Sight Locator Index

This index relates to the maps on the covers. We have given map references to the main sights of interest in the book. Grid references in italics indicate sights featured on the town plans. Some sights within towns may not be plotted on the maps.

LANZAROTE

Águila **2F**
Arrecife **7D**
Arrieta **11F**
Castillo de Santa Bárbara **7B**
Castillo de San Gabriel *Arrecife 4d*
Castillo de San José **7D**
El Charco de San Ginés *Arrecife 4a*
Costa Teguise **8C**
Cueva de los Verdes (Green's Cave) **11E**
Dunas de Corralejo **18H**
Ermita de los Dolores **5B**
Famara **7A**
Femés **3E**
Fundación César Manrique **7C**
El Golfo **2C**
Guinate Parque Tropical **10E**
Haría **10F**
Los Hervideros **2D**
Iglesia de San Ginés *Arrecife 4b*
Isla Graciosa **10C**
Istmo de la Pared **18R**
Islote de Hilario (Timanfaya) **3C**
Jameos de Agua **11E**
Jardín de Cactus **8B**
Mirador del Río **11D**
Monumento al Campesino and Casa-Museo del Campesino **6C**
Museo Agrícola el Patio **5B**

Orzola **11D**
Papagayo **3F**
Parque Nacional de Timanfaya **3C**
Playa Blanca **2F**
Puerto Calero **4E**
Puerto del Carmen **5E**
San Bartolomé **6C**
Salinas de Janubio **2D**
La Santa **5A**
Teguise **7B**
Uga **3D**
Valle de la Geria **4D**
Yaiza **3D**

FUERTEVENTURA

Antigua **16M**
Betancuría **15M**
Caleta de Fuste **17M**
Corralejo **17G**
El Cotillo **15H**
Ermita de Nuestra Señora de la Peña **14N**
Gran Tarajal **15Q**
Isla de Lobos **18G**
Jandía Peninsula **17S**
Monumento a Don Miguel de Unamuno **16K**
La Olivia **17J**
Pájara **14N**
Puerto del Rosario **17L**
Tefía **16K**
Tuineje **15P**

Index

Acknowledgements

The Automobile Association wishes to thank the following photographers, companies and picture libraries for their assistance in the preparation of this book.

Abbreviations for the picture credits are as follows – (t) top; (b) bottom; (l) left; (r) right; (c) centre; (AA) AA World Travel Library

4l Pleasure cruisers, AA/S Day; **4c** Era de la Corte hotel, AA/J A Tims; **4r** Parque Nacional de Timanfaya, AA/S Day; **5l** Volcanic scenery, La Geria, AA/C Sawyer; **5c** Charco de Sans Gines lagoon, AA/S Day; **6/7** Pleasure cruisers, AA/S Day; **8/9** La Rosita, Lajares, AA/J A Tims; **10/11** Promenade, Puerto del Rosario, AA/J A Tims; **10b** Puerto del Carmen, AA/J A Tims; **10br** Farmworker, AA/C Sawyer; **11c** Castillo de San Jose, AA/J A Tims; **11b** Goat, AA/J A Tims; **12bl** Castillo de San Jose, AA/J A Tims; **12br** Playa de los Verilitos, AA/J A Tims; **13t** Meal, Puerto de la Cruz, AA/J A Tims; **13c** Tapas bar, AA/C Sawyer; **13c** Fresh fish, AA/C Sawyer; **14t** Restaurant, Morro Jable, AA/J A Tims; **14b** Traditional Canarian meal, AA/J A Tims; **15t** Fresh fish platter, AA/J A Tims; **15c** La Geria vineyard, AA/C Sawyer; **15b** Malvasia Wine, AA/C Sawyer; **16** Geothermal demonstration, AA/J A Tims; **17** Montanas del Fuego de Timanfaya, AA/J A Tims; **18** Playa Papagayo, AA/S Day; **19c** Playa de Sotavento de Jandia, AA/S Day; **19b** Ferry, Orzola, AA/C Sawyer; **20/21** Era de la Corte hotel, AA/J A Tims; **25** Sunday Market, Teguise, AA/J A Tims; **27** Road, La Oliva, AA/S Day; **28** Bus, Corelejo, AA/S Day; **29** Two cyclists, AA/S Day; **34/35** Parque Nacional de Timanfaya, AA/S Day; **36t** Castillo de San Jose, AA/J A Tims; **36b** Castillo de San Jose, AA/J A Tims; **37** Castillo de San Jose, AA/C Sawyer; **38** Cueva de los Verdes, AA/J A Tims; **38/39** Cueva de los Verdes, AA/J A Tims; **40/41** Playa de Sotavento, AA/C Sawyer; **42/43** Fundacion Cesar Manrique, AA/S Day; **43** Fundacion Cesar Manrique, AA/S Day; **44/45** Parc Nacional de Timanfaya. AA/J A Tims; **46/47** Jameos del Agua, AA/S Day, © DACS 2007; **48** Jardin de Cactus, AA/J A Tims; **48/49** Jardin de Cactus, AA/J A Tims; **50/51** Isla Graciosa, AA/C Sawyer; **51** Isla Graciosa, AA/J A Tims; **52** Sunday Market, Teguise, AA/J A Tims; **53** Iglesia de San Miguel, AA/S Day; **54/55** Bogeda La Geria, AA/J A Tims; **56/57** La Geria, AA/C Sawyer; **59** Spa at Melià Volcán; **60** Isolte de Hilario, AA/S Day; **63** Caleta de Fustes, AA/C Sawyer; **64/65** Papagayo. AA/C Sawyer; **66/67** View from Isla de Lobos, AA/J A Tims; **68/69** View of Isla de Lobos, AA/J A Tims; **69** Isla de Lobos, AA/J A Tims; **70** Centro Insular de Artesania, AA/J A Tims; **73** La Lajita Dunes, AA/C Sawyer; **74** Boat trips, Corralejo, AA/J A Tims; **76/77** Morro de Jable, AA/C Sawyer; **78** Manrique Mobile, AA/S Day; **79** Manrique Mobile, AA/S Day; **80/81** Charco de Sans Gines lagoon, AA/S Day; **83** Orzola, AA/J A Tims; **84/85** Castillo de Santa Barbara, AA/C Sawyer; **86/87t** Playa de Jabillo, AA/J A Tims; **86/87b** Campo de Golf, Costa Teguise, AA/C Sawyer; **87** Playa Cuchara, Costa Teguise, AA/C Sawyer; **88** Kite Surfing, AA/J A Tims; **89** Parque Tropical Guinate, AA/J A Tims; **90** Flowers, AA/J A Tims; **91** Plaza de la Consitucion, AA/C Sawyer; **92/93** Graciosa Island, AA/S Day; **94/95** Isla Graciosa, AA/J A Tims; **97** Haria, AA/C Sawyer; **98/99** Orzola, AA/J A Tims; **109** Montana de la Cinta, AA/S Day; **110/111** Arrecife harbour, AA/S Day; **111** Castillo de San Gabriel, AA/S Day; **113** San Gines Church, AA/S Day; **114/115** Arrecife harbour, AA/S Day; **115** Promenade, Arrecife, AA/J A Tims; **116/117** Punta del Aguila, AA/S Day; **118/119** Ermita de las Dolores, AA/S Day; **118** Ermita de las Dolores, AA/S Day; **120** El Golfo, AA/S Day; **120/121** El Golfo, AA/S Day; **122** Los Hervideros, AA/S Day; **123** Casa Museo al Campesino, AA/S Day; **124/125** Villa Agricol el Patio, Tiagua, AA/S Day; **125** El Patio, Tiagua, AA/J A Tims; **126** Papagayo, AA/J A Tims; **126/127** Playa Papagayo, AA/S Day; **128/129** Parque Nacional de Timanfaya, AA/S Day; **129** Parque Nacional de Timanfaya, AA/S Day; **130** Parque Nacional de Timanfaya, AA/S Day; **130/131** Parque Nacional de Timanfaya, AA/C Sawyer; **131** Camel Ride excursion, AA/J A Tims; **132/133** Parque Nacional de Timanfaya, AA/S Day; **134** Mancha Blanca Visitors Centre, AA/S Day; **135** Isolta de Hilario, AA/J A Tims; **136/137** Playa Blanca, AA/J A Tims; **139** Puerto del Carmen, AA/J A Tims; **140/141** Puerto del Carmen, AA/J A Tims; **141** Puerto del Carmen, AA/J A Tims' **142** Plaza de los Remidios, Yaiza, AA/S Day; **143** La Geria, vineyards, AA/J A Tims; **144/145** Saltpans, Janubio, AA/S Day; **146/147** Uga, AA/J A Tims; **148/149** Uga, AA/S Day; **150** Yaiza, AA/C Sawyer; **163** Playa de Sotavento, AA/J A Tims; **164** Bogeda Santa Maria, AA/S Day; **165** Bogeda Santa Maria, AA/S Day; **166** Cruz de los Caldos Church, AA/J A Tims; **166/167** Santa Maria de Betancuria, AA/C Sawyer; **167** Bogeda Santa Maria, Betancuria, AA/J A Tims; **168/169** Caleta de Fustes, AA/C Sawyer; **169t** Monumento Al Marinero, Corralejo, AA/J A Tims; **169b** Playa la Clavellina, Corralejo, AA/J A Tims; **170t** Playa del Castillo, AA/J A Tims; **170b** Nuestra Senora de la Pena Church, AA/J A Tims; **170/171** Gran Tarajal, AA/J A Tims; **172** Isolte del Lobos, AA/S Day; **172/173** Morro Jable, AA/J A Tims; **174** Monument de Unamuno, Tindaya, AA/J A Tims; **175** Museo de Grano, La Oliva, AA/J A Tims; **176t** Igesia de la Virgen in Paraja, AA/S Day; **176b** Iglesia Nuestra Senora de la Regla, Paraja, AA/J A Tims; **177** Puerto del Rosario, AA/J A Tims; **178t** Ecomuseuo de la Alcogida, AA/J A Tims; **178b** Ecomuseo de la Alcogida, AA/J A Tims; **179** Tuineje, AA/J A Tims

Every effort has been made to trace the copyright holders, and we apologise in advance for any unintentional omissions or errors. We would be please to apply any corrections in any following edition of this publication.

Dear Reader

Your comments, opinions and recommendations are very important to us. Please help us to improve our travel guides by taking a few minutes to complete this simple questionnaire.

You do not need a stamp (unless posted outside the UK). If you do not want to cut this page from your guide, then photocopy it or write your answers on a plain sheet of paper.

Send to: **The Editor, AA World Travel Guides, FREEPOST SCE 4598, Basingstoke RG21 4GY.**

Your recommendations...

We always encourage readers' recommendations for restaurants, nightlife or shopping – if your recommendation is used in the next edition of the guide, we will send you a **FREE AA Guide** of your choice from this series. Please state below the establishment name, location and your reasons for recommending it.

_____
_____
_____
_____
_____
_____

Please send me **AA Guide** _____

About this guide...
Which title did you buy?

AA _____

Where did you buy it?_____

When? m m / y y

Why did you choose this guide? _____
_____
_____
_____
_____

Did this guide meet your expectations?

Exceeded ☐   Met all ☐   Met most ☐   Fell below ☐

Were there any aspects of this guide that you particularly liked? _____
_____
_____
_____

continued on next page...

Is there anything we could have done better? _____
_____
_____
_____

About you...
Name (*Mr/Mrs/Ms*) _____
Address _____
_____
_____ Postcode _____

Daytime tel nos _____
Email _____

Please only give us your mobile phone number or email if you wish to hear from us about other products and services from the AA and partners by text or mms, or email.

Which age group are you in?
Under 25 ☐   25–34 ☐   35–44 ☐   45–54 ☐   55–64 ☐   65+ ☐

How many trips do you make a year?
Less than one ☐   One ☐   Two ☐   Three or more ☐

Are you an AA member? Yes ☐   No ☐

About your trip...
When did you book? m m / y y   When did you travel? m m / y y

How long did you stay? _____

Was it for business or leisure? _____

Did you buy any other travel guides for your trip? _____

If yes, which ones? _____
_____
_____

Thank you for taking the time to complete this questionnaire. Please send it to us as soon as possible, and remember, you do not need a stamp (*unless posted outside the UK*).

AA Travel Insurance call 0800 072 4168 or visit www.theAA.com